Commentary on the
Gospel According to Matthew

Commentary on the
Gospel According to Matthew

John L. McKenzie

Foreword by
Emmanuel Charles McCarthy

WIPF & STOCK · Eugene, Oregon

COMMENTARY ON THE GOSPEL ACCORDING TO MATTHEW

Copyright © 2015 John L. McKenzie. All rights reserved. Except for brief quotations in critical publications or reviews, no part of this book may be reproduced in any manner without prior written permission from the publisher. Write: Permissions, Wipf and Stock Publishers, 199 W. 8th Ave., Suite 3, Eugene, OR 97401.

Wipf & Stock
An Imprint of Wipf and Stock Publishers
199 W. 8th Ave., Suite 3
Eugene, OR 97401

www.wipfandstock.com

ISBN 13: 978-1-60899-202-7

Manufactured in the U.S.A.

Contents

Foreword by Emmanuel Charles McCarthy | vii

Abbreviations | x

Introduction | xv

1　Prologue: Genealogy and Infancy Narratives (1:1—2:23) | 1

2　Book One: The Proclamation of the Reign (3:1—7:29) | 7

3　Book Two: Ministry in Galilee (8:1—11:1) | 33

4　Book Three: Controversy and Parables (11:2—13:52) | 51

5　Book Four: The Formation of the Disciples (13:53—18:35) | 71

6　Book Five: Judea and Jerusalem (19:1—25:46) | 94

7　The Passion Narrative (26:1—27:66) | 130

8　The Resurrection Narrative (28:1-20) | 148

Bibliography | 151

Foreword

JESUS, BEING A HUMAN being, does not grow up in a hermetically sealed vacuum. He is formed—as all human beings are formed—by previously formed human beings, within an existing culture complete with its own values, attitudes, beliefs, language(s), traditions, literature, superstitions and suppositions, postulates and presumptions. It is in the sacred Scriptures of the Jewish people—the texts Christians call the Old Testament—where we find the primary evidence for determining how the culture in which Jesus is formed came to be, what it is on its surface and in its depths. Each human being is by nature, of course, a unique person. But the uniqueness of each is inextricably tethered to the effect that the central nurturing institutions of a particular society has on him or her.

The Gospel of Matthew is the most Jewish of the four gospels. It is written for a Jewish audience, by a Jew, about a fellow Jew. It is suffused with the atmosphere, ideas, feelings, stories, hopes, truths, and metaphors of the Old Testament. For example, Jesus' Sermon on the Mount, while antithetical to many teachings in the Old Testament, did not and could not have entered the world in a culture nurtured in Greek myths and philosophies. By the same token, the Gospel of Matthew itself could not have arisen out of such a culture. Jesus, the Sermon on the Mount, and the Gospel of Matthew erupt from the lived history of a people and their encounters with the Holy One, *Yahweh*. The essential record of these encounters is captured in this people's sacred Scriptures.

It is from within this living and ongoing historical narrative that Jesus emerges and the Gospel of Matthew is composed. What Jesus thought, taught, and did is not the product of his sitting in the halcyon gardens of the Academy conceptualizing and re-conceptualizing the reality in which each human being lives and moves and has his or her being. What Jesus thought, taught, and did is the fruit of Biblical obedience: freely willing one thing in his thoughts, words, and deeds, and one thing only; namely, to do the will of *Yahweh,* whom he knew as *Abba,* Father.

Enter Rev. John L. McKenzie, author of this *Commentary on the Gospel According to Matthew.* By all standards of measurement McKenzie is a colossus among twentieth-century scholars of the Hebrew Scriptures. These are the Scriptures on which Jesus cut his spiritual wisdom teeth, and in which the author of the Gospel of Matthew—and the members of the Jewish-Christian community to whom he is writing—had been immersed since childhood.

The study of any text independent of its context generates at best dubious fruits and vulnerable "truths," if not outright falsehood perceived as truth. For example, most English-speaking people in contemporary culture know that the phrase "once upon a time" introduces a narrative whose content is not historical. In other languages, in other cultures, and at other times, such a phrase can introduce an historical event.

John L. McKenzie knew as much about the text on which and the context in which Jesus and the author of the Gospel of Matthew are formed as anyone on earth in the twentieth century. He brings this extensive and in-depth knowledge to his *Commentary on the Gospel According to Matthew,* the gospel in which the Old Testament is quoted more often than in any other book of the New Testament. His commentary is formed and informed by fifty years of Biblical scholarship, which includes writing several hundred scholarly articles on the Old and the New Testaments as well as highly acclaimed books of commentaries and interpretations on both Testaments (*The Two-Edged Sword, The Theology of the Old Testament, The Power and the Wisdom, The Old Testament Without Illusion, The New Testament Without Illusion,* and others)—and a nine hundred thousand-word *Dictionary of the Bible.*

One other work by Rev. John L. McKenzie—a further witness to his exceptional scholarship on the Hebrew Scriptures—bears considerably on the quality of his *Commentary on the Gospel According to Matthew.* This is his publication of a volume, titled *Second Isaiah,* in the venerable *Anchor Bible Series* for scholars. Isaiah is the second most-cited book in the New Testament, quoted fifty-one times. Only the Psalms are quoted more often (sixty-nine times), and no book comes in a close third. But equally significant to the quantity of quotations from Isaiah in the New Testament is the fact that Second Isaiah (Chapters 40-66 of the Book of Isaiah) contains the

Foreword

four "Servant of Yahweh" hymns, also known as the Songs of the Suffering Servant. In his *The Theology of the Old Testament*, McKenzie writes: "The fourth Servant Song is the major crux interpretum of the Old Testament. It is a completely new interpretation of the saving power and will of Yahweh." Second Isaiah is critical to a proper understanding of the progression of God's revelations of Himself and His will in the Old Testament and of the person and message of Jesus in the Gospel of Matthew.

In his interpretation of the New Testament, *The Power and the Wisdom*, McKenzie states,

> The early Church attributed the proclamation of this theme [Suffering Servant] to Jesus himself and no convincing reason has been urged to show it should be attributed to another. It is as deeply embedded in the Gospels as anything else. If this theme is not the work of Jesus himself then we know nothing about his words or person. The Suffering Servant theme is the peak of faith in the Old Testament, the supreme affirmation of the power of God and the weakness of man. When we meet the theme of the Suffering Servant as proclaimed in the New Testament, we are at the very center of the Christian revolution . . . We must point out, however, that mere animal pain does not save. Identity with Jesus suffering is first of all identity with Jesus loving.

If a person, Christian or non-Christian, is interested in knowing what the author of the Gospel of Matthew intended, or in knowing what the people who first read it or heard it understood by it, McKenzie's paragraph-by-paragraph—sometimes phrase-by-phrase or word-by-word—commentary will serve him or her well. Whether one's interest is intellectual curiosity, a search for truth, or finding a means of encountering the Jesus who was, and is, and always will be, he or she will discover all of that and more in John L. McKenzie's *Commentary on the Gospel According to Matthew*. For Christians or non-Christians spiritually starving to death on a non-nutritive or toxic daily diet of secular and religious superficialities and deceptions, this is a loaf of life-giving bread, created from the dough of undiluted and uncorrupted Gospel truth and made palatable and digestible by the hand of an inimitable master of his profession.

Emmanuel Charles McCarthy
August 31, 2013
Boston, Massachusetts

Abbreviations

Protocanonical and Deutrocanonical Books of the Bible

Old Testament

Gn	Genesis
Ex	Exodus
Lv	Leviticus
Nm	Numbers
Dt	Deuteronomy
Jgs	Judges
Ru	Ruth
1 Sm	1 Samuel
2 Sm	2 Samuel
1 Kgs	1 Kings
2 Kgs	2 Kings
Tb	Tobit
Ps	Psalms
Prv	Proverbs
Sir	Sirach (Ecclesiasticus)

Abbreviations

Is	Isaiah
Jer	Jeremiah
Dn	Daniel
Hos	Hosea
Am	Amos
Jon	Jonah
Mi	Micah
Zeph	Zephaniah
Mal	Malachi

New Testament

Mt	Matthew
Mk	Mark
Lk	Luke
Jn	John
Acts	Acts of the Apostles
Rom	Romans
1 Cor	1 Corinthians
2 Cor	2 Corinthians
Gal	Galatians
Phil	Philippians
2 Thes	2 Thessalonians
Jas	James
Ap	Apocalypse

Abbreviations

Apocrypha of the OT

QL Qumran Literature

Dead Sea Scrolls and Related Texts (QL)

    CD   Cairo (Geniza text of the) Damascus (Document)

    1QS   Serek ha-Yaḥad (Rule of the Community, Manual of Discipline)

Ancient and Modern Publications, Serials, Institutions

    AnalBib   Analecta biblica (Rome)

    Ant.   Josephus, *Antiquities of the Jews*

    APOT   R. H. Charles, *Apocrypha and Pseudepigrapha of the Old Testament* (2 vols.; Oxford, 1913)

    ASNU   Acta seminarii neotestamentici upsaliensis (Uppsala)

    Bl-Deb-F   F. Blass and A. Debrunner, *A Greek Grammar of the New Testament,* tr. R. W. Funk (Chicago, 1961)

    CBQ   *Catholic Biblical Quarterly*

    EDB   L. F. Hartman, ed., *Encyclopedic Dictionary of the Bible* (N.Y., 1963). English version of *BibLex*

    EvQ   *Evangelical Quarterly*

    EvT   *Evangelische Theologie*

    ExpT   *Expository Times*

    GrBib   M. Zerwick, *Graecitas biblica* (4th ed.; Rome, 1960). Numbers correspond to English tr., *Biblical Greek* (Rome, 1963)

    HarvTR   *Harvard Theological Review*

    HE   Eusebius, *Historia ecclesiastica*

    HeythJ   *Heythrop Journal*

    JBL   *Journal of Biblical Literature*

    JW   Josephus, *Jewish War*

Abbreviations

LumVi	*Lumière et vie*
NTB	C. K. Barrett, *New Testament Background: Selected Documents* (N.Y., 1961)
NTS	*New Testament Studies*
PCB	M. Black and H. H. Rowley, eds., *Peake's Commentary on the Bible* (rev. ed.; London, 1962)
QD	Quaestiones disputatae (English series; N.Y.)
RB	*Revue biblique*
Scr	*Scripture*
SPB	Studia postbiblica (Leiden)
Str-B	H. L. Strack and P. Billerbeck, *Kommentar zum Neuen Testament* (6 vols.; Munich, 1922-61)
ThDNT	G. Kittel, ed., *Theological Dictionary of the New Testament* (Grand Rapids, 1964—). English version of *ThWNT*
TRu	*Theologische Rundschau*
TS	*Theological Studies*
Wik, *NTI*	A. Wikenhauser, *New Testament Introduction* (N.Y., 1958)

Miscellaneous Abbreviations

Aram	Aramaic
Eng	English
Ep.	*Epistula* or Epistle
Fest.	Festschrift (generic name for *any* publication honoring a person)
Gr	Greek
Hebr	Hebrew
Lat	Latin
LXX	Septuagint (Greek translation of the OT)
ms(s).	Manuscript(s)

Abbreviations

MT   Masoretic Text (of the Hebrew Bible)

NT   New Testament

OT   Old Testament

Syn   Synoptic Gospels *or* Synoptic writers

Vg   Vulgate (common Latin version of the Bible)

Introduction

(I) Literary Character of the Gospel

THE OUTLINE OF MT [→ Introduction: (V) Outline] does not produce well-balanced parts. But the pattern of five books, if it exists, must be intended to suggest the five books of the Law. The outline would then reflect a theme that is clear in the Gospel without the outline: Jesus is the new Moses and the new Israel with a new revelation from God.

Compared to Mk and Lk, Mt is more obviously artificial, even contrived in its arrangement. This does not Mk and Lk are without artificiality in the arrangement; even Mark, who seems to be the most naïve and unstudied of the Evangelists, has arranged his narrative in an order other than the simple order of events. But Matthew apparently wishes to make it clear that his arrangement is his own. He uses a large number of "literary seams," lines intended to connect passages previously unconnected: His most common connecting particle, "at that time," usually has no temporal reference whatever. The discourses are clearly arranged as such, and each of the five major discourses is signified by an individual concluding formula. A synoptic table of the Gospels shows that most of the material in Mt's discourses is found in scattered contexts in Mk and Lk; and possibly the sayings that are peculiar to Mt were assembled by him from scattered contexts also. Each of the discourses revolves around a theme, as the outline indicates [→ Introduction: (V) Outline], except for the Sermon on the Mount; and the theme of this discourse is the righteousness of the Gospel as contrasted with the righteousness of the Law.

Introduction

Mt emphasizes the sayings of Jesus both in discourses and in narratives. This interest in his teaching is in sharp contrast to Mk; the same interest appears in Lk, and Jn is almost entirely a report of the discourses of Jesus. The development of interest is obvious here; but Matthew has his own interest in the teaching. In Mt Jesus is contrasted with the scribes, the teacher of Judaism; he is a teacher far superior to them—a new Moses, as we have noted. Mt is as much a presentation of Jesus' teaching as it is a recital of his life; and the primitive form of the Gospel was a proclamation of the life, passion, death, and resurrection of Jesus. K. Stendahl has attributed Mt to a group of Christian scribes, "the school of St. Matthew," who wished to produce a handbook of Christian conduct to be used by teachers. Such a handbook would fill in the Christian community the place that was occupied by scribal teaching in the Jewish community. Thematic grouping of material appears not only in the discourses but also in the narratives; the pieces in 8:1—9:34 focus upon the revelation of Jesus as Messiah and the confession of his messiahship. The numerical groupings may also have a pedagogical purpose, although a symbolism of number is not excluded. There are seven petitions in the Lord's Prayer, seven parables in the parable discourse, seven woes against the Pharisees, and three temptations. Sayings and narratives are sometimes connected by catchwords, a mnemonic device.

Mt is written in good Greek, superior to that of Mk; but a conscious effort to write good Greek is seen more clearly in the narratives than it is in the discourses and sayings, which more frequently reflect an Aram source. But Mt also shows features of Semitic style; he employs synonymous and antithetic parallelism (7:24–27; 16:25), repetition of formulas, and strophic structure (5:3–10; 12:22–32). These cannot all be attributed to an Aram source with equal probability; the Evangelist was sufficiently versed in Semitic style to be able to combine it with Greek.

The schematism of the Gospel as a whole is also reflected in details. It can be seen that Mt usually abbreviates the miracle narratives of Mk. A definite pattern can frequently be discerned: introduction of the persons, the request, the reaction of Jesus, command and effect, and the reaction of the spectators. Matthew's writing here loses some of its vitality and results in a dry and monotonous style; this is not because Matthew does not know how to write vividly. By contrast Mark's vividness is in some ways artless. Matthew strives for a hieratic recital in which the miracle becomes a clear epiphany of divine power exercised without effort. When the heavenly

Introduction

reality is manifested, the event is detached from space and time. In Mt the transfiguration of Jesus has begun.

It is no accident that the words of Jesus are quoted more frequently from Mt than from any other Gospel. The Evangelist was deeply interested in Jesus' teaching; he presented the teaching in a compressed economical style that allows the impact of the sayings to be felt with no loss of power. This is not to imply that the sayings of Jesus are feebly recounted in the other Gospels, but simply to give to Matthew the credit for careful composition he so fully deserves. It can be noticed in the commentary that we are not concerned with the question which Gospel reports more accurately "the very words" of Jesus; this question admits to no answer. The form of Mt's sayings often reflects beyond doubt the experience of the primitive Church and its meditation on the person and the words of Jesus. Matthew is an excellent spokesman for this experience and meditation. It is paradoxical that, in spite of the force of his style, he has sometimes recast sayings that in Mk's form were too harsh for his readers.

(II) Relation of Mt to the Other Synoptic Gospels

The Syn theory adopted in this commentary is the simplest and most widely accepted theory. In spite of the difficulties involved, this theory raises fewer problems than any of the more detailed theories that have been proposed. But its adoption here does not imply that it is a final solution; it must be considered subject to revision, and therefore any conclusions that rest upon it should be considered provisional.

The theory can be simply outlined. It supposes that Mk is the earliest of the Syn, and that Mk was used as a source by both Matthew and Luke; and this means Mk in the form in which we now have Mk. It supposes that neither Matthew nor Luke knew each other. The large amount of material that only Mt and Lk have in common is not attributed to any form of interdependence, but to their use of a common source, usually called Q, from the Ger word *Quelle*, "source." If the common parts of Mt and Lk that do not appear in Mk are combined into a single document, this document would not be a gospel; and it is not supposed that Q was a gospel. But one of the difficulties in this Two-Document Hypothesis is the problem of defining what kind of document Q was. A document must be presupposed, in the opinion of the great majority of critics; the resemblances between Mt and Lk are too close verbally to be explained as having derived from a common oral tradition. That there was oral tradition before the Gospels or Q were written is doubted by no one; but the problem of the relationships of the Gospels is a literary one.

Since Q was not a gospel, it is usually assumed that it was a collection of the sayings of Jesus. Such collections appear in the *Pirqe Aboth* and also in Gk literature. However, scrutiny of the Q passages reveals at once that Q was not a collection of isolated aphorisms, like Prv in the OT. The community of Mt and Lk shows that the sayings must have been woven into connected discourse in at least some of the passages. This part of the hypothesis again is not altogether satisfactory, but attempts to multiply this documentary source into several sources have been no more satisfactory.

Besides Mk and Q, Mt has material found in no other Gospel. Since Mk and Q are documentary sources, many critics postulate a third document for Mt's material (often called M). This document cannot be considered a gospel, nor is it a collection of sayings; Mt has narrative passages peculiar to itself. Whether such a written source need be postulated for Mt's own material is not as clear as the postulate of Q; for Q is postulated because of a clear literary relationship. Effectively the symbol M designates nothing except material that is neither Mk nor Q; the character of M or proto-Mt simply cannot be determined. There is no convincing reason why this material may not be stray pieces of oral tradition first put in writing by Matthew.

The Evangelist's method of handling his sources can be traced only for Mk. The method can be described in two paradoxical qualities: Mt is dependent on Mk; and Mt is very free in the use of Mk. Where Mt follows Mk, it can be said generally that it betrays the use of no other source. The expansions are few, and almost without exception they admit an explanation that is based on Mt's theological conceptions. It follows the order of Mk closely, but allows some rearrangements that again can be explained by its theological purpose. The general structure—baptism, Galilean ministry, miracles, controversy, confession of Peter, predictions of the passion, journey to Jerusalem, Jerusalem controversies, passion, resurrection—is not substantially altered. At the same time Mt is free in its use of Mk. The exercise of this freedom is most obvious in the abbreviation of narrative passages, usually by the omission of descriptive details. Mt makes little use of the dialogue that occurs in Mk; personal names are generally not retained. Conversely, Mt shows no independence of Mk in its geography; Mt, which has been alleged to be "Palestinian," is much more vague on the

Introduction

geography of Palestine than is Jn, which has so long been attributed to a Hellenistic Christian (or an ex-Palestinian resident of Ephesus).

The sayings of Mt, both its own and those derived from Q, are inserted without dislocating the narrative of Mk. Most of them occur as mass insertions. Where Mk has sayings, Mt by rearrangement of the context sometimes gives them a different turn. This also is an example of freedom; the alterations we find need not be attributed to theological intentions. Some sayings certainly appeared both in Mk and in Q, but in a slightly different form in each. We can easily suppose that other variant forms of the sayings were in circulation, and Matthew felt free to adopt that particular form and context best suited to his purpose.

It is not entirely certain that we can project Matthew's handling of Mk into the handling of his other sources, e.g., Q.

Because of Matthew's interest in Jesus' teaching, it may be a poor presumption that he treated the sayings that came to him in the same manner as the narratives of Mk. Certainly he did not regard Mk's sayings as immutable formulas; not infrequently he couched them in a form he considered better. He could have shown the same freedom combined with dependence toward Q that he shows toward Mk, but we have no reason to assert that he treated Q with less freedom than he applied to Mk. For the sayings peculiar to Mt we have no point of reference at all; but if the Evangelist allowed himself liberty in his use of the other sources, it seems improbable that he denied himself liberty here.

(III) The Theological Character of the Gospel

Matthew, we have noted, has been called a Christian scribe or rabbi. The designation means that he (or the school that he represents) instituted the same kind of study of the Gospel that the scribes of Judaism made of the Law. The parallel should not be pressed too closely; there is a world of difference between Mt and the Talmud. Nevertheless, there are points of contact between Mt and the rabbinical writings that are not found in the other Gospels. These points of contact are more than an interest in the Law and allusions to Jewish institutions. Matthew sometimes moves in the world of rabbinical thought. He not only is familiar with rabbinical dialectic; he uses it. He describes genuine rabbinical discussions. Certainly nothing in this implies undue liberty with the traditions. If Jesus was recognized in any character in the Jewish community, it was as a rabbi. That he engaged

Introduction

in rabbinical arguments and discussions is certain; but the other Gospels are less familiar with this world of thought than Mt, and they report it in less detail. These methods are employed by Matthew because he wishes to make a point that is directed toward Judaism: the thesis that Jesus Messiah is the new Moses and the new Israel, and the fulfillment of the Law and the Prophets. This thesis, which could only be directed to a Jewish audience, is supported by the type of argument accepted in Jewish learning. Mt reflects not only the rabbinical discussions of Jesus himself, but controversies of Jewish Christians with their fellow Jews.

Matthew cites the OT 41 times. Of these quotations 21 are common to Mk and Lk, and evidently Mk is the source. But 20, nearly half his total, are not found in Mk and Lk; and 10 of these 20 are found in no other NT book. Here we enter an area where Matthew shows his greatest originality. Of the 41 texts 37 are introduced with a formula; the most common formula is "that it might be fulfilled." Matthew's idea of fulfillment is treated in the commentary on 1:22; it is not the idea of the fulfillment of a prediction, but of the growth of a reality to its destined fullness. There is a certain rough similarity between Matthew's use of OT texts and the type of midrashic interpretation found in QL (see J. A. Fitzmyer, *NTS* 7 [1960-61] 297-333).

The source of these quotations is a matter of interest. Some are quoted according to the LXX, some according to the MT, and some according to neither of the two. That Matthew (or the other authors) used either the MT or the LXX at random or always quoted from memory seems highly improbable. Several scholars have postulated a handbook of OT texts devised for the use of Jewish Christians from which it could be argued that Jesus is the Messiah of the OT (cf. J.-P. Audet, *RB* 70 [1963] 381-405). The existence of such a handbook would explain the lack of consistency in the texts that are quoted in one Gospel or in all the Gospels taken together. Matthew may have supplemented the texts of such a handbook by some he gathered himself; or he may simply have used more of the texts given than Mark did.

Mt is called a Jewish Christian Gospel, and in this it differs from Mk and Lk; the allusions to Judaism and the use of the OT are a part of this pattern. The central theological purpose of Mt is to show that Jesus is the Messiah of the OT. The Jews should have recognized him, but they did not; and the messiahship of Jesus emerges against a background of Jewish unbelief and hostility. Jesus is Son of God and Son of David. The humanity of Jesus is transfigured by softening the emotional reactions attributed to Jesus in Mk and by the hieratic style of the miracle stories. In these details Jesus does not appear less human but as a man with a mysterious and superior personality. Matthew retains a number of the texts in which the "Messianic Secret" of Mk appears, but he continues his Gospel after these passages as if they had not occurred. Jesus is transparently the Messiah in Mt, and only willful unbelief can obscure this truth. The obtuseness of the disciples to the messiahship of Jesus, a basic theme in Mk, is softened by Matthew; again he keeps a number of Mk's texts, but continues with his own material in such a way that the disciples appear to have a good understanding of the messiahship, if not a complete one. In this respect Matthew has certainly retrojected the faith of the apostolic Church into the Gospel narrative; but in spite of this it is the faith of the apostolic Church that his Gospel proclaims.

Jesus is Messiah, but not the king Messiah of popular expectation. Mt identifies him as the suffering Son of Man whose saving work is accomplished through his passion and death. He is the lowly Messiah, a friend of the poor because he is one of them. Jesus renounces wealth and power and calls upon his disciples to do the same. He has no political message; only Mt has the verse in which Jesus says that those who take the sword shall perish by the sword. The reign comes with Jesus, but it is not a reign of the king Messiah over a Jewish world empire. The reign is accomplished by free submission to the sovereign will of God.

Mt is a Jewish Gospel, but it is also a Gospel of the Church. The reign of God in Mt is clearly identified with the community of the disciples, a community that is identified with Jesus himself. Mt has not the Pauline idea of the body or the Johannine idea of the vine, but Jesus is present where two or three assemble in his name, and he remains with the disciples until the eschatological consummation. Mt's reign is universal. The unbelief of the Jews has opened the Gentile world for the proclamation of the Gospel. The Gentiles are not evangelized simply because of the defect of Jewish faith; Matthew understands that Israel should have proclaimed its Messiah to the world, but has refused to accept him. For the Church is the new Israel, and because the Church alone believes in Jesus Messiah it is the only true Israel. The "fulfillment" of Israel must be realized in the Gentile world without the people of Israel.

But the reign of God is not identified with the Church in such a way that the identification is total. The reign of God is fulfilled only in an eschatological event. Here Mt does not differ from Mk; Mt's contribution is the eschatological thrust of the Christian community. The eschatological event

Introduction

begins with the Church. And indeed the rejection of the Messiah by the Jews initiates the eschatological mystery; this rejection elicits the judgment, which in Mt 24 is merged with the eschatological judgment.

Since Jesus is the Messiah of the OT, Matthew finds it necessary to state the position of Jesus toward the Law, the basis of Judaism in NT times. This position is expressed in a classic phrase: Jesus did not come to destroy the Law, but to fulfill it. To fulfill the law means to bring it to the fullness of which it is a developmental phase. The reign—and Jesus himself is identified with the reign—is this full reality. Jesus is lord of the Law; he does not annul it any more than mature manhood annuls childhood, but the "yoke" of the reign removes the yoke of the Law. Jesus reduces all the commandments of the Law to the commandment of love; love is Christian freedom. Love communicates not a lesser righteousness, but a greater; and when the reign has arrived the Law is no longer righteousness.

In this context the controversy between Jesus and the Pharisees is not a controversy between Jesus and the Law. The Pharisees do not represent the true Law; they do not teach and observe the true Law, for they do not recognize that it demands its fulfillment in the Messiah. They have attributed to the Law a sufficiency it does not possess and have maintained its efficacy by adding to it the traditions of men. Jesus flatly rejects the Pharisaic thesis that the Law in its totality included "the traditions of the elders." These traditions have made the Law an intolerable burden. The Pharisees have reduced the union of man with God to a carefully fixed set of routine external observances and have thus reduced righteousness to a man-made product. In effect, they deny man's sinfulness because they do not confess guilt for real sin; they polish the outside of the vessel, but their interpretation of the Law does not touch the heart.

In the development of these themes Mt reflects the controversies of Christians and Jews in the apostolic Church; but very possibly it also reflects discussions within the Jewish Christian community. It is clear from Acts and the Pauline epistles that the problem of the Gospel and the Law was the central theological problem of the first generation of the Church. Mt has its place in this discussion; and in spite of the fact that it is called the Jewish Gospel, Mt's thesis on the Law is the same as the thesis of Paul in substance, although it is couched in different terms.

INTRODUCTION

(IV) Authorship, Date, and Place of Composition

There is no evidence that Mt ever bore any other title or attribution. Nor has there been any doubt that the Matthew meant is the tax collector whose call is related in Mt 9:9-13 and who is enumerated in the lists of the Twelve. There are, however, certain problems here; the name of the tax collector in Mk 2:13-17 and Lk 5:27-32 is Levi, and it must be assumed that Levi (like Simon Peter) had a change of name. Jews did not bear two Semitic names. The Gk *Matthaios* represents the Hebr *Mattai*, abbreviated from *Mattityāhû* or *Mattanyāhû*. The assumption of a change of name is not too difficult; no Levi appears in any of the lists of the Twelve.

The first attribution of literary work to Matthew is the statement of Papias, bishop of Hierapolis in Phrygia *ca.* AD 130, quoted by Eusebius in the 4th cent. (*HE* 3.39,16); the statements of Irenaeus and Origen are probably dependent on Papias (Wik, *NTI* 179-81). Papias does not call the writing of Matthew a gospel, but says that "Matthew collected the sayings [Gk *logia*] in the Hebr language and that each one translated [or interpreted?] them as best he could." The "sayings" are generally understood to mean the sayings of Jesus; and this work would have borne some resemblance to Q. But the *logia* may mean a collection of OT texts, a handbook of texts for apologetic use of the type described above. Irenaeus and Origen speak not of *logia* but of a gospel; and there is no doubt that they meant the Gospel we know.

The text of Papias is open to many questions. Eusebius did not regard him as well informed, and the passages that have survived in quotations indicate that his information—not to say his thinking—was more than slightly confused. There is no evidence that Papias saw the Aram (which he calls Hebr) document to which he refers. There are no citations of the Aram M anywhere in early Church literature. The question of whether Matthew wrote the Gospel that bears his name is thus closely connected with the question of the original language of Mt. If Matthew is not the author of an Aram gospel, it does not follow that he wrote no gospel; but the only ancient literary testimony is that Matthew wrote in Aramaic.

That the canonical Gk Mt is not a translation of an Aram original is universally accepted by scholars. It can be retranslated into Aramaic no more easily than Mk or Lk. Its Greek is superior to that of Mk. It contains a number of wordplays (6:16; 21:41; 24:30) possible only in Greek. The 21 OT quotations found in Mt, Mk, and Lk are given according to the LXX; in the quotations peculiar to Mt the Hebr text is followed more closely but with affinities to the LXX, and the indications are that Matthew did not use the MT for these quotations. They may come from a handbook of the type previously mentioned. Matthew's dependence on Mk for his narrative passages is clear beyond doubt; and of special pertinence here is Matthew's dependence on Mk in the story of the call of Matthew—a passage that in the hypothesis of the authorship of Mt must be autobiographical. If an Aram M existed, it would not be the exact original of the present Gk Mt: the Gk Mt would have to be such a substantial and thorough rewriting as to eliminate all traces of the original. If Matthew was the author of the Aram M, he cannot be the author or translator of the Gk Mt.

The case for an Aram M was ably presented by M.-J. Lagrange, and is at present upheld by P. Benoit. Most scholars do not find the arguments for it convincing, for the reasons indicated above; the doubts can be summed up simply in the absence of any trace of the existence of an Aram M except for the quotation of Papias and the use of Papias by writers who depended on him. If the Gk Mt is the original Gospel—and everything suggests that it is—then it cannot be attributed to the tax collector Matthew, one of the Twelve. There is nothing to suggest the personal identity of the author.

Irenaeus alone of the early writers suggests a date; he makes the authorship of Mt contemporaneous with the preaching of Peter and Paul in Rome—i.e., before AD 68. This detail cannot be tested. Internal evidence suggests (but does not demonstrate) a date later than the fall of Jerusalem in AD 70. But the familiarity of the author with Palestinian Jewish customs does not allow us to remove the Gospel—in space or in time—too far from Palestinian Judaism before the Jewish rebellion. It is not without interest that Matthew's acquaintance with Jewish customs and practices is not matched by acquaintance with Palestinian geography; his geography lies mostly in Galilee, and Matthew, as a Palestinian Jew, need not have known Galilee. But if the Gospel was written later than AD 70, there are excellent reasons for thinking that it was written outside Palestine. Many scholars suggest Antioch in Syria, a city where Jewish and Gentile Christianity met and mingled, and where the questions of the relations of the Law and the Gospel were very probably acute. The material peculiar to Mt is best explained as drawn from Palestinian traditions directly; and this would have been possible in Syria.

Introduction

(V) Outline

To outline Mt or any of the four Gospels might appear to be a simple task; but commentaries on Mt show a surprising diversity in their conceptions of the plan and outline. This diversity is ultimately due to the Evangelist, who in this as in other respects is more subtle than he seems: the plan of the book is a part of his purpose. This commentary is arranged according to the commonly accepted scheme of five books; but not all interpreters think this is the guiding plan, and this approach presents difficulties. That is, the discourse against the Pharisees, which is nearly as long as the missionary discourse, is not treated as a separate discourse; nor is the eschatological discourse counted in the number. But since the discourses are obvious points of division and are easily recognized, this scheme has been adopted here.

(I) Prologue: Genealogy and Infancy Narratives (1:1—2:23)
   (A) The Genealogy of Jesus (1:1-17)
   (B) The Birth of Jesus (1:18-25)
   (C) The Worship of the Magi (2:1-12)
   (D) The Flight into Egypt and the Slaughter of the Innocents (2:13-23)
(II) Book One: The Proclamation of the Reign (3:1—7:29)
   (A) Narrative Section: The Beginning of the Ministry (3:1—4:25)
   (B) Discourse: The Sermon on the Mount (5:1—7:29)
(III) Book Two: Ministry in Galilee (8:1—11:1)
   (A) Narrative Section: Cycle of Ten Miracles (8:1—9:34)
   (B) Discourse: The Missionary Sermon (9:35—11:1)
(IV) Book Three: Controversy and Parables (11:2—13:52)
   (A) Narrative Section: Incredulity and Hostility of the Jews (11:2—12:50)
   (B) Discourse: The Parables of the Reign (13:1-52)
(V) Book Four: The Formation of the Disciples (13:53—18:35)
   (A) Narrative Section: Various Episodes Preceding the Journey to Jerusalem (13:53—17:27)
   (B) Discourse: The Sermon on the Church (18:1-35)
(VI) Book Five: Judea and Jerusalem (19:1—25:46)
   (A) Narrative Section: Journey to Jerusalem and Events There (19:1—23:39)
   (B) Discourse: The Eschatological Sermon (24:1—25:46)
(VII) The Passion Narrative (26:1—27:66)
(VIII) The Resurrection Narrative (28:1-20)

Introduction

Further subdivisions of the Gospel will be found in the commentary itself.

Chapter 1

Prologue

Genealogy and Infancy Narratives (1:1—2:23)

MT AND LK BOTH have accounts of the conception and the birth of Jesus and of some incidents that followed the birth. Neither Mk nor Jn touch upon this period of the life of Jesus. The genealogies of Jesus found in both Mt and Lk are not parallel, nor are there parallels elsewhere in their Gospels. It is difficult to reconcile some of the details in the accounts of Mt and Lk. The absence of the infancy narratives in Mk suggests very strongly that these narratives did not exist in the earliest form of the Christian traditions about Jesus and that various traditions about the infancy were formed later. Mt's version of the traditions is greatly affected by the use of OT texts. Theological imagination and symbolism also play a very large part in the composition of the infancy narratives.

(A)The Genealogy of Jesus (1:1-17)

The purpose of the genealogy is to show that Jesus is the Messiah (1:1,16), the term of the history of salvation that was begun with the promises to Abraham. Mt here takes the view of the E source of the Pentateuch, which also begins with Abraham; Lk, like the J source (Lk 3:23-38), begins with the first man. Jesus is king Messiah, the son of David, and Messiah of Israel, the son of Abraham.

The genealogy is deliberately compiled in 3 sets of 14 names (1:17); 14 is a multiple of 7. It is divided at the two critical points of Israelite history, the foundation of the monarchy of David and the collapse of the monarchy of Judah in the Babylonian conquest of 587 BC. The artificiality of the numbers is maintained by the omission of the names of Ahaziah, Jehoash, and Amaziah between Jehoram and Uzziah; the queen Athaliah was regarded as a usurper, and she would not have figured in the genealogy in any case. Mt follows the line of the kings of Judah; Lk follows a cognate line. Mt's genealogy up to Zerubbabel could be formed by copying from a text of OT books; for the rest of the genealogy, there is no documentary source with which we can compare it.

Four women appear in the genealogy: Tamar, Rahab, Ruth, and Bathsheba. No principle governs their inclusion. Tamar deceived her father-in-law Judah into an incestuous union (Gn 38). Rahab in folklore was the prostitute of Jericho who sheltered the spies and was admitted to the Israelite community (Jos 2). Ruth, the heroine of the Book of Ru, was a Moabite who joined the Israelite community. Bathsheba was the wife of Uriah and the partner of David's adultery. The only common element (probable, but less clear for Bathsheba) is that they were foreigners.

The number 14 in the third group can be maintained only by including Mary or by counting Jesus and Christ as two; it is possible that a name was omitted in the early transmission of the text. One could explain the inclusion of Mary because of the virgin birth, clearly declared in the following passage. If Jesus and Christ are counted as two, the duality could be understood as referring to his nativity in the flesh and to his Second Coming; such an eschatological allusion is common in Mt. 10. *Amos:* This reading of the critical text stems from an early confusion of the name of King Amon with the name of the prophet Amos.

The reconciliation of the divergent genealogies of Mt and Lk already was a celebrated problem in patristic times. Reconciliation assumes that both genealogies are compiled from reliable records. It is known that genealogies were kept in the post-exilic Jewish community, but this does not prove that genealogies were available to Matthew and Luke. It is much simpler to suppose that each genealogy was compiled artificially where the biblical record failed or where Luke, for reasons of his own, chose not to follow the line of the kings of Judah.

Prologue: Genealogy and Infancy Narratives (1:1–2:23)

(B) The Birth of Jesus (1:18-25)

In this and the following section some noteworthy differences between the narratives of Mt and Lk appear. Joseph is the central and the active figure in Mt. He is the recipient of revelation, which comes to him through the appearance of an angel in a dream. Mt mentions no residence in Nazareth prior to the birth. It agrees with Lk in the statement of the virgin birth and in the childhood residence of Jesus in Nazareth. 18. *espoused:* The written contract of marriage had been drawn up between Joseph (or his parents) and the parents of Mary. The Jewish marriage ceremony was accomplished when the groom took the bride into his house; this is meant by "come together" (1:18) and "take" (1:20,24). Premarital unchastity in these circumstances was not adultery in the full sense of the word, nor was the repudiation of a marriage contract "divorce" (1:19) in the full sense of the word. It is very doubtful that the rigorous, capital penalty of the Mosaic Law and the talmudic traditions was enforced in NT times. 19. *righteous:* Joseph is called thus because of his desire to observe the Law. This righteousness was united with an unwillingness to expose his wife; it lay within his power to repudiate the agreement by signing a declaration in the presence of witnesses, but without stating the reasons in public. 20. *the angel of the Lord:* A messenger figure of the OT (e.g., Gn 16:10; 22:11,15–16; Ex 3:2; Jgs 6:13; 2 Sm 24:16; cf. *EDB* 87–90). The angel of the Lord announces the birth of Samson (Jgs 13:3). Here he announces the name of the child: Jesus. The Gk form *Iēsous* represents the Aram *Yēšuaʽ* and the Hebr *Yᵉhōšûaʽ*. According to a popular etymology the name means "Yahweh is salvation"; this child will be an agent of salvation but the people will be saved from their sins, not from external enemies or dangers from nature. The greatest to bear this name in the OT was the hero of the Book of Joshua.

22. *might be fulfilled:* Matthew presents the event as the fulfillment of Is 7:14. The formula of "fulfillment" occurs 11 times, more often than in the other 3 Gospels combined. The term does not signify mere prediction and fulfillment; and it is difficult to state in modern terms the kind of thinking involved. The saving event of the Gospel gives the word of the OT, which is a declaration of the power and will of God to save, a new dimension of reality. The text of Is is quoted according to the LXX, except for the reading "they shall call" (LXX: "you shall call"; MT: "she shall call"). 23. *virgin:* The LXX used *parthenos*, "virgin," to translate the Hebr word in Is 7:14 for "young girl" (*ʽalmāh*). This gives the text of Is a new dimension of reality, and Matthew uses it to affirm the virgin birth. His emphasis, however, seems to be

more on the declaration of a savior who shall be called Emmanuel, "God is with us," than on the word *parthenos*. The birth initiates the Messianic age of salvation to which the whole OT looks forward. The age begins with the birth of a child, and this is the force of the allusion to Is. Jesus realizes the presence of God among his people in an entirely new way. 25. *until she had borne a son:* This verse has caused trouble since the early heresies of the Helvidians and the Jovinians, who concluded from it that Mary and Joseph had marital relations after the birth of Jesus. The implication, easily taken in English, is not present in the Gk particle *(heōs),* and still less if we suppose a Semitic background of the passage. The NT knows nothing of any children of Mary and Joseph. Matthew's interest here is in the affirmation that Joseph is not the natural father of Jesus, and his language is determined by this interest. The agent of the conception of Jesus is "a Holy Spirit" (1:20). This term is used in the OT to designate God's mysterious power; it is not used to designate the agent of human conception.

(C) The Worship of the Magi (2:1-12)

1. *in the days of King Herod:* One of the rare chronological pieces of information in Mt places this event in the time of Herod the Great, a satellite king of Judea (37–4 BC). It is impossible to date the year of the birth of Jesus exactly; according to the reckoning of Dionysius Exiguus, Herod the Great died four years before Jesus was born. *Magi:* The visitors are called *magoi* (Lat *magi,* whence the Eng term); it is probably used in a loose sense. Originally the term designated the learned priestly caste of the Persians; later it came to mean any one skilled in occult knowledge and power (much the same as our "magician," which is derived from the same word). It could also mean a mountebank or charlatan. Matthew certainly does not use the word in an abusive sense. The mention of the "star" shows that they are called *magoi* because of their knowledge of astrology. Nothing else is said about them. *from the east:* This suggests Mesopotamia, the home of astrology in the Hellenistic world. The story reflects the popular belief that each person is represented by a star, which appears at his birth. 2. *his star:* It is impossible to identify a particular heavenly body as the star of Bethlehem; any attempt to do so would be futile. Although the allusion is not explicit, the Jewish reader would recognize the star that rises from Jacob (Nm 24:17)—an allusion to David usually interpreted in a messianic sense.

Prologue: Genealogy and Infancy Narratives (1:1—2:23)

The story of the Magi, like the genealogy of Jesus, affirms that Jesus is king Messiah. The Magi seek a king, and Herod consults the religious experts of Judaism to find out where they should look. Of this there is no doubt; they should look not in Jerusalem but in Bethlehem. 5. *in Bethlehem of Judea*: The place of David's birth and the place of origin of the king Messiah of the future. In support of this the text of Mi 5:1–3 is cited. The text is cited neither according to the LXX nor according to the MT; it is conflated with the text of 2 Sm 5:2 (the offer of kingship made to David by the elders of Israel). 7. *the time of the appearance of the star*: The inquiry about the time looks to the sequel in 2:13–23. No guidance of the star is suggested for the journey prior to the arrival of the Magi in Jerusalem; but now it leads them not only to the town but to the very house. 11. *gold, frankincense, myrrh*: The gifts that the Magi bring echo Ps 72:10; Is 60:6. The dream motif recurs; the Magi are warned not to return to Herod.

The theme of the story is not only the royal messiahship of Jesus but also the adoration of him by the Gentiles. In contrast to Luke, who places Jewish poor at the scene of the nativity as the first to worship Jesus, Matthew puts the Gentiles first, and the Jews, even when informed of the birth, remain indifferent. This is a theme that is echoed several times throughout the Gospel.

(D) The Flight into Egypt and the Slaughter of the Innocents (2:13–23)

The dream motif recurs again both in the departure to Egypt and in the return. 15. *out of Egypt*: The quotation of Hos 11:1 (according to the MT) illustrates the freedom with which Matthew employs the OT. The original refers to the "call" of the Exodus. Jesus is presented as re-enacting in his own life the career of Israel; for he is the new Israel. 18. *a voice heard in Ramah*: Jer 31:14 is quoted with similar freedom; the quotation follows neither the LXX nor the MT exactly. The original text refers to the destruction of the monarchy of N Israel by the Assyrians in 721 BC. The confusion of Ephrath in the territory of Benjamin with Bethlehem is as old as the gloss on Gn 35:19. A Moslem shrine just N of Bethlehem, identified with the tomb of Rachel, reposes on an early tradition.

19. *when Herod had died*: The return from Egypt is dated after the death of Herod (4 BC). Herod's kingdom was divided by Augustus among three of Herod's surviving sons, Archelaus (Judea, Samaria, Idumea),

Herod Antipas (Galilee and Perea) and Philip (the territory to the E and N of Galilee). At the petition of the Jews Augustus denied the title of king to Archelaus and gave him the title of ethnarch. His government was so unsatisfactory that he was deposed and exiled to Gaul in AD 6. The warning given to Joseph in a dream explains why Jesus, although born in Bethlehem, was reared in Galilee and was known as a Galilean. Lk, which agrees with Mt both on Bethlehem and Galilee, explains the relation of the two places in a different way: Joseph and Mary were originally residents of Galilee and were only temporary visitors to Bethlehem when Jesus was born. 20. *they that sought the child's life:* The influence of the OT appears in this phrase; it is taken almost verbally from Ex 4:19. 23. *spoken by the prophets:* The text of "the prophets" quoted is found nowhere in the OT. Nazareth is not mentioned in the OT. The most probable explanation of the "quotation" is that it is a wordplay based on the Hebr text of Is 11:1, "A shoot shall rise from Jesse, and a branch (*neṣer*) shall sprout from his roots." There is an assonance between the word neser and the town name Nazareth.

The tragic episode of the Innocents is mentioned in no other literature, canonical or profane; this raises serious questions about the historical character of the incident. Such a wanton action is in harmony with the character of Herod as Josephus has described it (*Ant.* 15.3,3 § 53–56). Josephus depicts Herod as being pathologically jealous of his power—a number of his family were murdered by him because he suspected them of trying to supplant him. There is no doubt that Josephus meant to paint Herod as black as he could, and it is difficult to explain the absence of the Bethlehem incident in Josephus except on the hypothesis that he knew nothing about it. That he should have omitted it because of its interest for Christians is unlikely; Josephus has demonstrated his ability to write history according to his own ends. Therefore it should be considered that the incidents of ch. 2 possibly represent a symbolic presentation of the royal messiahship of Jesus and the opposition of secular power to this messiahship. The opposition finally achieved its purpose in the passion of Jesus. This type of theological narrative is supported by the use of OT texts.

Chapter 2

Book One

The Proclamation of the Reign (3:1—7:29)

(A) Narrative Section: The Beginning of the Ministry (3:1—4:25)

(a) The Preaching of John the Baptist (3:1-12)

THE FIRST SIX VERSES of this passage follow Mk 1:1–6 closely, adding only the location in the desert of Judea (3:2) and the content of the preaching of John. 1. *wilderness of Judea:* The desert of Judea is the steep slope that falls from the central ridge of the country to the valley of the Jordan and the Dead Sea. Baptism in the Jordan indicates that John preached near the river, very probably not far from Jericho. This is only a few miles distant from Qumran, and the relations of John to the Qumran sect offer occasion for interesting speculation (see J. A. T. Robinson, *HarvTR* 50 [1957] 175–91). 2. *repent, for the kingdom of heaven is at hand:* The sentence in which John's preaching is summarized is identical with the summary of the proclamation of Jesus in 4:17. 3. *this is he:* The mission of John is described in all three Gospels by the text of Is 40:3, quoted according to the LXX, and no doubt originally in Mk. Mt omits Mk's conflation of Mal 3:1. Mt, like Mk, introduces John abruptly; only Lk has the story of John's nativity. John the Baptist was a well-known figure in the early Christian community who needed no introduction; disciples of John appear even at Ephesus (Acts

19:1–5). 4. *garment of camel's hair:* John's residence in the desert and his garb and diet suggest the prophet Elijah (2 Kgs 1:8); see the question of the return of Elijah in 11:14; 17:10–12. 6. *were baptized by him:* Mt does not use Mk's phrase, "baptism of repentance for the remission of sins"; possibly by the time of Mt this phrase might have seemed to assimilate the baptism of John to Christian baptism; but see 3:11. Mt alone (3:14–15) expresses the difficulty about the reception by Jesus of a rite that involved repentance and remission.

Mt 3:7–10 (Lk 3:7–9 par.) comes from Q. Mt limits these words to the Pharisees and Sadducees; Lk directs them to the whole crowd. 7. *brood of vipers:* The epithet occurs also in 12:34; 23:33. This suits Mt's general pattern; the religious leaders of the Jews are responsible for the refusal of the Jews to believe in the Messiah. The words of John are strongly eschatological, reflecting the "coming wrath" of the Day of the Lord (Am 5:18–20; Zeph 1:14–16). 9. *from these stones:* The threat alludes to the rejection of the Messiah by the Jews and his acceptance by the Gentiles; the Church of Jews and Gentiles is the new Israel and the true people of God. 10. Cf. 7:19. 11–12. These verses contain the Messianic preaching of John, expanded by Mt from Mk; 3:12 (Lk 3:17 par.) is from Q. To Mk's baptism with a Holy Spirit Mt and Lk both add "with fire"; this seems to be an allusion not only to fire as the element that symbolizes the presence of the deity, but also to the appearance of the Holy Spirit in tongues of fire in the Pentecost narrative. "The spirit of truth" as purifying water appears in 1QS 4.21 (see J. A. T. Robinson, *HarvTR* 50 [1957] 175–91). The fire in the expansion of Q (3:12) is the destroying fire of Gehenna. It is clear from the importance of John both in Judaism and in primitive Christianity that his messianic witness was of great value. Some apparently were ready to take John as the Messiah; John himself disclaimed this office, and pointed to another. The complete witness of John is given later (11:2–6).

(b) The Baptism of Jesus (3:13–17)

Matthew depends on Mk, but has added 3:14–15—it was necessary to explain how Jesus could submit to a rite of repentance and confession of sin. 15. *a fulfillment of all righteousness:* An obscure phrase; it very probably refers to Jesus' identification of himself, as he comes to be baptized, as a devout Jew who observes the Law and the practices associated with good Jewish life. The added dialogue introduces a confession of the dignity of

Jesus by John not found in Mk and Lk. 16. *the spirit of God descending:* In Mt and Mk, Jesus sees this event as the heavens open, but in Lk and Jn 1:32-33 the vision is extended to John (at least). *a dove:* Here only the symbol of the Spirit; in OT imagery the dove represents a symbol of love. 17. *this is my beloved son:* Love is expressed in the saying formed on Is 42:1 (following Mk). The use of this formula identifies Jesus as the Servant of the Lord. The vision defines the character of the messiahship of Jesus; he is not the royal conquering Messiah but the Servant who proclaims and suffers.

The "voice from heaven" reflects the Jewish belief in the *bat qôl* (daughter of a voice), often mentioned in rabbinical literature as the means of revelation granted after prophecy had ceased (Str-B 1, 125-34).

(c) The Temptation of Jesus (4:1–11)

Mk's brief notice of the 40 days' fast in the desert and temptation is expanded by Mt (and Lk) into a triple temptation. A common documentary source for Mt and Lk is not obvious; if there is a common source, one of the two Evangelists has handled it freely. The biblical quotations (from the LXX) are identical in the two Gospels. The order of the second and third temptations is inverted in Lk from Mt; the order of Mt seems to have a deliberately arranged climax. The movement of Jesus to the desert occurs under the guidance of the Spirit. 1. *into the desert:* This area is not specified; probably the desert of Judea (see 3:1) is intended. Jebel Qarantal, named after the 40 days, lies to the W of Jericho and is traditionally associated with the mount of temptation. 2. *forty days:* This phrase suggests the 40 years of Israel in the desert. The desert sojourn was a time of temptation and failure for Israel; but Jesus, the new Israel, is likewise tempted in the desert. The symbolic character of the narrative is evident; the temptations and Jesus' answers define the true character of his Messianic mission. The answer of Jesus to all three questions is taken from Dt (8:3; 6:16,13). The use of this source shows that the Law itself reveals the true character of messiahship.

The three temptations can be summed up as temptations to power. The first temptation is to use miraculous power to provide for ordinary material needs. 4. The answer of Jesus (Dt 8:3) does not deny that ordinary needs should be met by ordinary means, but subordinates even basic physical necessities to the revealed word of God. Jesus does not fulfill his mission by providing for basic physical necessities, but by proclaiming the word that is life.

5. The second temptation also deals with miraculous power; it is the use of this power to produce a "sign" (12:38–42), a spectacular and convincing display that would compel belief. This type of sign Jesus does not give. *the pinnacle of the temple:* It has not been certainly identified. If the ancient structure of Herod's temple had relations to the topography similar to those of the modern Haram esh-Sherif, the SE corner of the esplanade lay well above the level of the slope of the valley of Kidron; this may be the point meant. 6. Here the tempter supports his proposal with a biblical quotation (Ps 91:11–12). 7. Jesus responds by quoting Dt 6:16, a warning against rashness. The appeal to the spectacular sign imposes demands upon God that God has not promised to fulfill; it is not the way in which he has chosen to reveal himself. 8. *a very high mountain:* The mountain of the third temptation does not exist in nature. This is a temptation to secular messianism, the use of political power to accomplish the ends of the Messianic mission. 10. Jesus' answer to this temptation exceeds his previous answers in severity and is prefaced by a dismissal. The quotation of Dt 6:13 places secular messianism on the level of the worship of false gods.

The temptations of Jesus all touch upon his Messianic mission; even in a theologically symbolic narrative Jesus is not represented as liable to the common temptations of mankind. Nor in the mind of the Evangelist is he really subject to the temptation to abuse his Messianic powers. The temptation comes not to him but to the Church, which carries on his mission. The elaboration of the temptation story by Matthew has an ecclesial purpose. The spiritual dangers that threaten the integrity of the mission of the Church have already been met by Jesus himself; he has shown how the Church must overcome them.

(d) The First Proclamation in Galilee (4:12–17)

The complete account of the imprisonment of John the Baptist is given in 14:1–12. The three Syn (and Jn in its own way) agree that Jesus did not begin his own proclamation until John had been imprisoned by Herod Antipas. The associations of Jesus and John are too obscurely known for us to determine what is implied in this situation. The Syn, as we have seen, do not relate any confession of John the Baptist in any way similar to the version we find in the Fourth Gospel. We may conjecture that the preaching of John had aroused a climate of interest into which Jesus could move with his own proclamation. All three Syn also agree that Jesus returned

BOOK ONE: THE PROCLAMATION OF THE REIGN (3:1—7:29)

to Galilee, his own country, to proclaim the reign. 13. *in Capernaum by the sea:* Jesus moved from his own village of Nazareth to the larger city of Capernaum (identified with the ruins Tell Hum near the northern end of the western shore of the Sea of Galilee). In NT times the western shore of the lake was occupied by many busy and prosperous small cities and towns; and we must assume that Jesus wished to reach a wider audience. *in the territory of Zebulun and Naphtali:* Matthew notes that Capernaum lay in the old tribal territory of Zebulun and Naphtali; this enables him to adduce Is 8:23—9:1 (LXX 9:1-2). In the Isaian passage deliverance of 9:2-6 is first announced to the territory of Galilee, which was detached from the kingdom of Israel by Tiglath-pileser III of Assyria in 734 BC and erected into an Assyrian province. The first part of Israel to experience the destroying wrath of Yahweh shall be the first to hear of his salvation. The quotation follows neither the LXX nor the MT.

17. *kingdom of heaven:* Mt compresses Mk's summary of the proclamation of Jesus, using the phrase Mk uses to summarize the preaching of John (3:2) without Mk's allusion to the "time" (*kairos*) and Mk's call to faith. The typical Matthaean phrase, "kingdom of heaven," appears here instead of Mk's "kingdom of God"; the circumlocution of "heavens" for "God" was a common Jewish manner of speech. Jews of this period avoided the use of the divine name or what were regarded as peculiarly divine titles. The word usually translated "kingdom" is more accurately rendered "reign"; this is the word employed in this commentary, except in a few passages. The word does not designate an area in which power is exercised, but the exercise of the power. What "approaches" (or "is arriving") is the manifestation of the supreme power of God, the assertion of his sovereignty. The first response to this is repentance; for sin is a refusal to accept the reign of God.

(e) The Call of the First Disciples (4:18-22)

Matthew here depends on Mk, which he has slightly rewritten. Luke, perhaps employing a peculiar source, has rewritten the story more extensively and added the miraculous catch of fish. Jn 1:35-42 has a quite different account: Andrew and another disciple (not named, but presumably John himself) were disciples of John the Baptist, who introduced them to Jesus; and Andrew introduced his brother Simon. The point of the story in Mt and Mk is that the four followed Jesus immediately even though they did not know him; they "dropped" their fishing nets, left their families, and became disciples. There is no implication that they returned to their homes and their livelihood. Three of this first four—Peter, James, and John—formed an inner three who witnessed incidents not seen by the other disciples (17:1; 26:37; Mk 5:37). A similar urgency is expressed in the call of Levi (9:9). The promise to make them "fishers of men" is an intimation of the apostolic office.

(f) A Journey in Galilee (4:23–25)

This brief passage is compiled by Matthew as an introduction to the first of his major discourses, the Sermon on the Mount. The summary is described in commonplaces: teaching in the synagogues (mentioned several times), proclaiming the good news of the reign, healing diseases, exorcising demons. As a result of these activities Jesus became known "in all Syria" (4:34). The Roman province of Syria was bounded by the Taurus mountains, the Syrian desert, the Nabataean kingdom, and the Mediterranean. Matthew means those parts of the province mentioned in 4:25; Galilee, the Decapolis (N and E of Galilee), Judea and Perea (E of the Jordan). These are regions which Jesus traversed. The region of Tyre and Sidon (Mk 3:8; Lk 6:17) is not mentioned, very probably because Matthew thought that this territory was already included in his enumeration; see 15:21.

(B) Discourse: The Sermon on the Mount (5:1—7:29)

1. *the mountain:* Jesus is meant to be the new Moses proclaiming the new revelation on a new Mt. Sinai. Much of the sermon is paralleled in Lk, but the extensive discourse, which contains most of the parallels, is strangely given not on a mountain but in a plain (Lk 6:17). The preceding narrative has gathered the crowds (5:1) that hear the sermon. The discourse is introduced with unusual solemnity; Matthew means this to be the explication of what he has called the proclamation of the reign or the good news of the reign.

(a) The Beatitudes (5:3–12)

3. *blessed are:* Or "happy is the one who . . . " This formula is common in Pss and in OT wisdom literature; it also appears elsewhere in other NT

Book One: The Proclamation of the Reign (3:1—7:29)

books, and in particular in Ap. The beatitudes as such are not attributed to Q; Lk 6:21–24 has four beatitudes and four woes. Lk's beatitudes are parallel to Mt's first, second, fourth, and the expansion of the eighth (see below). The woes of Lk are antitheses of the beatitudes. The beatitudes of Mt are "spiritualized" in comparison to those of Lk, emphasizing the quality of virtue and the activity of virtue; Lk speaks of poverty, hunger, and mourning. *poor in spirit*: The difference between Lk's "poor" and Mt's "poor in spirit" is not substantial; Mt certainly does not mean those who, although they are wealthy, are spiritually detached from their wealth. The phrase very probably echoes Is 61:1 (see Lk 4:18). Both phrases designate the poor class, which constituted the vast majority of the population of the Hellenistic-Roman world. In later OT literature and in the literature of Judaism the name of this class, ʾanāwîm or ʾaniyyîm (frequently confused because of the similarity of spelling), became almost a technical term for devout and observant Jews. Mt's "poor in spirit" emphasizes less the literal lack of possessions than the lowly condition of the poor; their poverty did not allow them the arrogance and assertiveness of the wealthy but imposed habitual and servile deference. The term is very close to "meek" in the third beatitude. Their reward is "the kingdom of heaven"; in this context "kingdom" rather than "reign" is meant.

4. *those who mourn*: If 5:3 echoes Is 61:1, 5:4 very probably echoes Is 61:2; to console the mourners is one of the functions of the messenger who speaks in this passage of Is. The beatitude at least means those who have no worldly joy, and in this sense would be closely parallel to the first and the third. More probably it means those who mourn the evils of Israel, which are due to its sins. Their consolation will be the experience of the Messianic salvation. 5. *the meek*: These are the same class as that designated in 5:3, the lowly who are unable to be aggressive. The ideal of meekness is described concretely in 5:39–42. *the land*: The meek shall possess the eschatological land of Israel, restored by the saving deeds of God. The phrase echoes the promises of the land to the OT patriarchs. 6. *who hunger and thirst for righteousness*: The "righteousness" after which one should hunger and thirst is a word of broad meaning. In Mt it most frequently designates the condition of good relations with God—achieved by submission to his will. In Pharisaic Judaism this condition was thought to be assured by the observance of the Law according to Pharisaic standards. Jesus insists that his disciples must strive for something higher than this (5:20). "Righteousness" can also

echo the OT idea of the victory of God over his enemies, his vindication of himself and of Israel. The reward is to obtain what is desired.

7. *the merciful:* The ideal of mercy or compassion is a frequent theme in all the Gospels. The beatitude is illustrated by the parable of the merciless servant (Mt 18:23–35). The two works of mercy most emphasized in Mt are almsgiving and forgiveness. The reward of compassion is to receive compassion. 8. *the pure of heart:* Purity of heart is opposed to the external Levitical purity achieved by ritual ablution: this is a frequent object of contention between Jesus and the Pharisees. What is meant by purity of heart is explained in 15:10–20. It is manifested principally by speech, which betrays one's thoughts and desires. The reward of purity of heart is to see God. This does not signify what in theology is called "the beatific vision," but admission to the presence of God (see 18:10). In OT language the members of the royal court are those "who see the face of the king." 9. *the peacemakers:* This word does not represent the Hebr phrase, "one who produces prosperity," but means those who reconcile quarrels. Reconciliation is a Christian office often recommended in the Gospels; see 5:23–26. The reward is to be called sons of God. This is a title of Israel in the OT; those who reconcile quarrels are genuine Israelites.

10–12. In spite of the repetition of "blessed" in 5:11, the number of beatitudes is eight, not nine; the beatitude is expanded in 5:11–12. Persecution for righteousness is persecution that is endured in order to maintain good relations with God by obedience to his will (see comment on 5:6). The expansion identifies Jesus with righteousness. He replaces the Law as the one and the sure means by which one maintains good relations with God. This relationship will certainly bring persecution (described in terms of the experience of the primitive Church), but the reward is greater than any reward promised before. The Church is the successor of the prophets, who were persecuted by their own people; the persecution mentioned is most probably the attacks made on the Christian community by the Jews.

It is difficult for us to appreciate the paradoxical character of the beatitudes. They institute a moral revolution that has not yet reached its fullness. They are opposed to all the conventional values of the Jewish and the Hellenistic-Roman world and pronounce blessings on those who do not share in these values. Not only the external values of wealth and status are repudiated but also those goods of the person that are achieved and defended by self-assertion and strife. The general statements of the beatitudes are enlarged by concrete examples in the following passages of the sermon.

BOOK ONE: THE PROCLAMATION OF THE REIGN (3:1—7:29)

(b) The Salt of the Earth and the Light of the World (5:13–16)

The function of the disciples is illustrated by the homely metaphors of salt as seasoning and the single lamp that was used in the one-room house of the Palestinian peasant. The explanation of the two images (5:16) refers them to the "good works" of the disciples. By living according to the teaching of Jesus, men will manifest the goodness of "their father in heaven" (a common phrase in Mt) and will praise God because of what they see. This is very probably the original force of the images. In Mt's text the image is expanded by the possibility of the loss of savor of salt and the hiding of the light under a measure; he who fails to realize the ideal of the life of the Gospels will be rejected. The related idea of the city on the mountain, which is not explained, appears to be a popular wise saying that is intruded into the context, something like the Eng simile "stands out like a sore thumb." In the context of the sermon these sayings serve as an introduction to the lengthy passage that follows; here the disciples are instructed in the manner in which they can become the salt of the earth and the light of the world, and what the good works are through which God is glorified.

(c) The Law and the Gospel (5:17–48)

In the initial encounter of the Gospel with Judaism, as well as in those primitive churches that were entirely or largely Jewish in membership, the attitude of Jesus and the Church to the Law was an urgent question. The Law had a sacredness and a saving value in Pharisaic Judaism that do not perfectly reflect the place of the Law in pre-exilic Israel. The Law was thought to be the summary of all wisdom—human and divine, the revelation of God himself, a complete and a secure guide of conduct and endowed with a sacramental assurance of good relations with God. This value of the Law Jesus did not and could not accept; implicitly for most Jews the Law was the terminal revelation of God.

The attitude of the NT books toward the Law is not homogeneous. This does not mean that it is inconsistent, but simply that it reflects the development of the Christian understanding of the Law and its relation to the Gospel. One can trace the uneasy stages of this development in the epistles of Paul. A certain superficial inconsistency could be found, if one wished to be captious, even in 5:17–20, and much more easily in the entire Sermon on the Mount. To affirm inconsistency ignores the subtlety and the complexity of the problem, as well as the historical conditions in which Jesus proclaimed the gospel. This introductory pericope is Matthew's effort to state Jesus' position toward the Law in general. It must be read with the rest of the Gospel in mind.

17. *not to annul*: It was not the mission of Jesus to annul (break down, as a camp) the Law and the Prophets; these two words are often used to designate the whole collection of the books of the OT, and they are so used here. His mission is to "fulfill" them. *Fulfill*: This word cannot refer to a simple literal observance; the following six examples negate such a facile interpretation. "Fulfill" means to bring the Law to perfection, to give it that finality the Pharisees believed it possessed. Jesus affirms indirectly that the Law is imperfect, unfinished; he will perfect and finish it. In popular messianism the Messiah had a relation to the Law, but it was not a relation of bringing the Law to completeness. Jesus affirms the enduring, even eternal reality of the Law that we find affirmed in the rabbinical writings; but it is the finished and perfect Law that endures, not the Law of Moses with its explanatory oral teachings. 18. *Amen*: In this affirmation Jesus uses the asseverative *Amen* so common in the Gospels. There is no parallel to this use of the word. It usually expresses agreement with a statement or a wish, particularly a prayer; Jesus uses it as an asseverative particle of his own words. *jot*: The Hebr consonant, *yodh*, the smallest of the 22 consonants in the late or square Hebr script. *tittle*: Lit., "little horn"; it is less certain in meaning, but probably designates the small decorative "horn" added to many Hebr consonants in the square script. *until all things be done*: A deliberately obscure phrase; the Law will not pass until it has been finished and perfected by the Messianic work of Jesus.

19. Jesus accepts the rabbinical distinction between "heavy" and "light" commandments; the rabbis counted 613 distinct precepts in the Pentateuch and classified them according to their seriousness. From the terms "great" and "small" the words of praise and condemnation are derived. This again is not a program of literal Pharisaic observances; in fact, it is most probably the Pharisees who are meant by those who teach and practice nonobservance; see 15:3–6; 23:16–26. The nonobservance by Jesus of the traditional Sabbath ordinances and of the laws of Levitical cleanliness was a frequent source of controversy. Jesus is not recommending here that which he repudiated in teaching and practice. The Law therefore that the disciples are to "do and teach" is again the perfect and complete law. Observance of the Law and the traditions will secure the righteousness of

Book One: The Proclamation of the Reign (3:1—7:29)

the scribes and Pharisees; this righteousness will not gain admission to the reign. The righteousness of the disciples must exceed the righteousness of the scribes and Pharisees; it is a submission to the will of God that goes beyond the observance of the Law. What this departure from the Law means is illustrated in the following six examples (5:21–48). Paul also speaks of a righteousness of the Law that is not true righteousness and does not save; true righteousness is achieved through faith in Christ Jesus (Rom 3:20; 10:5; Gal 2:16; 3:21; Phil 3:9). For Matthew also, faith is that which saves.

(i) Murder (5:21–26)

In each of the six examples that follow, the statement of the Law (not distinguished from its explanation in tradition) is directly opposed to the pronouncement of Jesus: "I say." The statement of the Law is impersonal; the quotations are not attributed to God himself. This may reflect Jewish delicacy in speaking of the deity, and it also avoids an antithesis between the words of God and the words of Jesus. 21. *you shall not kill:* The commandment is quoted according to Ex 20:15; Dt 5:18; the added statement concerning the judgment is not a quotation from the OT, but judicial processes for murder are mentioned (see Ex 21:12; Nm 35:16–33). Jesus does not distinguish between willful murder and casual homicide (Ex 21:13; Nm 35:10; Dt 19:4–6), for accidental homicide does not fall under moral consideration. 22. *anyone who is angry:* What Jesus prohibits is not murder but anger; and the mere feeling of anger is liable to the court's judgment, a procedure that in the Law follows murder. There is an element of hyperbole; anger is not the object of legal action. Jesus rather means that anger, the passion that impels to murder, is as guilty an action as murder itself. The Law is restated. Expressions of anger in speech without violent action are reprobated in even stronger language. There is a climax in the penalties; the words move from the *krisis*, the judgment (which probably designates the local court), to the *synedrion* (council, Sanhedrin), the supreme legal body in Judaism, to the *gehenna* of fire, the final punishment God inflicts. No similar climax can be perceived in *raka* and *mōre*. Raka (probably =Aram rēqā, found as an abusive term in the Talmud) means "fool," "empty-headed," and can scarcely be distinguished from the Gk *mōros*. Efforts to find a climax in the terms, or to discover some particularly insulting quality in *mōros*, are fallacious; interpreters are deceived by the severity of Jesus, and they cannot believe that he speaks so sternly of simple abusive language.

The point is that the two words have no peculiar force beyond that of colloquial abusive terms like "idiot," "blockhead," "numbskull," "stupido," "Dummkopf," and their equivalents in all languages. It is just this type of language as an expression of anger that Jesus totally forbids. He strengthens the prohibition of murder by going to the very roots of mutual dislike.

23. Should men yield to anger, which is conceived as unavoidable, the sacred duty of reconciliation arises. The directions in 5:23–24 go as far as possible to make clear the urgency of this duty. Worship was to a Jew the most sacred action in which a man could engage. But worship must be postponed for reconciliation. The primacy of fraternal relations over cultic duties is established beyond all doubt; and this again is a restatement of the Law. The case in 5:23–24 is not the case of one who feels anger but of one who has excited anger in another; it is irrelevant to the duty of reconciliation who started the quarrel.

25–26. This saying is found in Lk 12:57–59 in an eschatological context; and it is probably original in this context. *your adversary*: In the context of Lk it is most probably not the brother with whom one has a dispute, but God, whose judgment the sinner is in danger of incurring. By transferring the saying to this context Mt has altered its meaning. He makes of the saying an expansion of the commandment of reconciliation, in which the element of urgency is again expressed. The eschatological threat adds to the severity of the commandment; but it is scarcely possible to overstate the sternness that Jesus everywhere voices toward those who refuse to love.

(ii) Adultery (5:27–30)

27. *you shall not commit adultery*: The commandment is quoted according to Ex 20:13; Dt 5:17. Jesus does not attend to the penalties prescribed in the Law for adultery, which was normally a capital crime (Dt 22:22). Neither does he mention illicit sexual relations that are not adulterous, although these are treated of in the Law. 28. *looks with lust*: As in the discussion of murder, the supreme offense is taken as the point beyond which Jesus advances. The statement is brief; the gaze of lustful desire is as guilty as the adulterous action. The lustful gaze is mentioned very frequently in the rabbinical literature, and it is reprobated with scarcely less vigor than we find in the Gospel passage (Str-B 1, 298–301). The restatement of the Law is directed again at the roots of the impulse. 29–30. The expansion in these verses is found also in 18:8–9, in a form that shows more clearly the

BOOK ONE: THE PROCLAMATION OF THE REIGN (3:1—7:29)

dependence of Mt on Mk 9:43–48. Mt has detached the saying from its original context, in spite of the fact that the hand is less relevant to the topic than the eye. The passage is rewritten for the present context. (On scandal, see comment on 18:6–9.)

(iii) Divorce (5:31–32)

See also 19:9; Mk 10:11–12; Lk 16:18. **31.** *whoever divorces his wife:* The statement of the Law is a very loose paraphrase and compendium of Dt 24:1, omitting the phrases that deal with the occasion of the divorce—the wife does not find favor with her husband because he has found "something shameful" in her. The meaning of this obscure phrase was extensively discussed by the rabbis. Rabbinical tradition tells of two governing views in NT times: the opinion of Shammai, who permitted divorce only for adultery, and the opinion of Hillel, who permitted divorce for the love of another woman or for causes as trivial as inferior cooking (Str-B 1, 312–20). The law of Dt actually deals only indirectly with divorce; its object is the prohibition of the reunion of partners after a divorce. **32.** *everyone who divorces his wife:* The saying was found in Mk and Q, and Matthew used both sources. The clarity of the saying in Mk and Lk is undisputed; there Jesus simply forbids divorce entirely. Mk's formula reflects Roman law, which allowed the wife to institute divorce; Mt and Lk allude to the Jewish practice, in which only the husband could divorce. *except the case of unchastity:* This exceptive clause is universally regarded as an expansion of the original form. Many interpreters and the Greek church understand it as a permission of divorce for adultery. But this is so plainly out of harmony with Mk and Lk that it seems improbable. Mt is the only Gospel that seems to allude to the rabbinical disputes; the allusion is quite clear in 19:3 (see comment). The interpretation of the phrase as an exception to the repudiation of divorce would place Jesus with the school of Shammai. If Matthew meant adultery, he chose a less apt word for it; *porneia* means literally "prostitution," and it designates unchaste conduct generally. *Moicheia* (the cog. word occurs in 5:32) means "adultery." The distinction between the two words is not so rigid as to make it impossible that here *porneia* means adultery. Nevertheless, if the verse is translated "He who dismisses his wife, except for adultery, makes her commit adultery," the saying sounds quaint, to say the least; the divorced wife commits adultery unless she has already committed adultery. J. Bonsirven (*Le divorce dans le Nouveau Testament* [Tournai, 1948]) called attention to a rabbinical use of the Hebr word z*e*nūt, which would be translated by the Gk *porneia*, to designate an unlawful union of concubinage. He proposed that it was this type of union that was designated by the exception. It is easier to understand this interpretation if one recalls that Greek has no distinct noun for "wife." Literally the sentence reads: "Every one who sends away his woman—except in the case of concubinage—makes her commit adultery." This seems to be the most satisfactory interpretation of the passage, and it explains the exceptive clause from the Jewish background that is so often apparent in Mt. (For another explanation of *porneia*, see comment on Mk 10:12.)

(Isaksson, A., *Marriage and Ministry in the New Temple* [ASNU 24; Lund, 1965]. Richards, H. J., "Christ on Divorce," *Scr* 11 [1959] 22–32.)

(iv) Oaths (5:33–37)

33. *you must not swear falsely:* The statement of the Law is not a direct quotation, but a paraphrase of such passages as Ex 20:7; Lv 19:12; Nm 30:3; Dt 23:22. The statement in Mt's paraphrase does not distinguish vows and oaths; it prohibits perjury and commands that vows be paid. 34. *do not swear at all:* In particular Jesus forbids the type of evasion that substitutes for the divine name something less sacred. If a sacred object is mentioned in an oath, it is as if the divine name were being used. The identity of such objects with the deity is shown by quotations from Is 66:1; Ps 47:3 (quoted according to the LXX). 36. *by your head:* Nor should one swear by one's self. All of the formulas mentioned in this verse, except "by Jerusalem," are attested in biblical or extrabiblical Jewish literature (Str-B 1, 330–36). A simple affirmative or negative is sufficient; more than this is "from evil." 37. The ambiguity of the Greek permits this last phrase to be rendered either "from evil" or "from the evil one"; see 5:39. In either translation the meaning is the same; the oath is a reflection of the evil condition of man, exhibiting both his mendacity, against which the oath is thought to protect, and his distrust of his fellow man.

The passage is echoed rather closely in Jas 5:12. Like the other antitheses, the statement is paradoxical. The prohibition of perjury is intended to secure truthfulness in situations where a solemn affirmation or denial is demanded. In the new ethics of Jesus truthfulness will be secured not by an oath but by the inner integrity of the person. The oath, because of its

Book One: The Proclamation of the Reign (3:1—7:29)

implications of mendacity and lack of confidence, can have no place in a society that does not assume evil as a matter of course.

(v) Revenge (5:38-42)

38. *an eye for an eye:* The law of retaliation is quoted loosely from Ex 21:24; Lv 24:20; Dt 19:21. The law of revenge was an ancient custom of the Near East that protected individuals by obliging the next of kin to avenge injury or murder or to purchase property to pay the debts of a kinsman. The laws of the Pentateuch are actually restrictions that limit the injury inflicted by the avenger to injury proportionate to the damage done by the aggressor. 39. *do not resist the evil one:* The customary principle of self-defense is rejected by this saying of Jesus; and the customary principle is not replaced by another principle of self-defense. The saying is probably the most paradoxical of all the sayings of the passage and has certainly been the object of more rationalization than any other. The statement is simply not to resist "evil" or "the evil one"; in the context it seems that the person rather than the neuter is meant, and we almost think of "the evil one" as the aggressor. *if anyone strikes you:* Several concrete examples are given that take the saying out of the mere abstract and general. The first area is the area of physical violence, which is not to be met with physical violence; it is to be suffered. 40. The second area is that of legal contention; the disciples are told not to meet legal action with legal action, but to yield what is contested and even beyond what is contested. The garments mentioned are the tunic, a long shirt worn next to the body, and the cloak, a heavier outer garment that protected against cold and rain. These were normally the only two garments worn by the Palestinian peasant. In Ex 22:25-26 the creditor who takes the cloak in pledge is directed to return it at sundown so that the debtor may have covering for the night. 41. The third area is that of forced labor or service, a part of the contribution of the subjects of ancient states to the government. 42. The fourth area is that of requests for gifts or loans, which are not to be refused. It is difficult to see how the principle of nonresistance and yielding could be more clearly stated. The rationalizations of the words of Jesus do not show that his words are impractical or exaggerated, but simply that the Christian world has never been ready and is not ready now to live according to this ethic. The passage is echoed in Rom 12:17-21; see also 1 Cor 13:5-7.

(vi) Love of one's enemies (5:43–48)

43. *love your neighbor:* The precept of the love of one's neighbor is quoted from Lv 19:18; the precept of hating one's enemy is not found in the OT, nor is it a summary of rabbinical teaching as it has been preserved (Str-B 1, 353–68). It no doubt represents the popular understanding of the love of one's neighbor; no one needs to be instructed to hate his enemies (cf. M. Smith, *HarvTR* 45 [1952] 71–73). The saying should not be restricted to personal enemies among one's brotherhood, implying a toleration of hatred of the enemies of one's group; this would not distinguish the Christian from the Gentile or the tax collector (5:46–47). The "neighbor" is the member of one's group or fellowship: one's village or town, one's religion or nation, one's tribe or race. In many languages the same word is used to designate "stranger," "foreigner," or "enemy." The enemy is specified in Mt as the persecutor, probably a reflection of the experience of the early Church; Lk has "those who mistreat you" (6:27). 45. *be sons of your Father:* The disciples are to show the same indifference to friends and enemies that God shows in his distribution of sunshine and rain; in exhibiting this godlike providence they vindicate their title of sons of God. Love within one's group or fellowship is merely a natural and universal human trait; Mt uses terms that identify two despised classes among the Jews: the Gentiles and the tax farmers. The use of these terms is something of a lapse from the principle Mt is stating; elsewhere the Gospel is friendly to these despised classes; see 9:10; 11:19; 21:31. By this kind of love the disciples will be perfect as the heavenly Father is perfect. 48. This verse is conflated from Dt 18:13 and Lv 19:2, where the word "holy" is used. "Perfect" represents the Hebr word for "whole" or "integral"; it is the love of one's enemies that assures the integrity of Christian morality and distinguishes it from merely ethical morality. This passage also is echoed in Rom 12:17–21.

(d) Genuine and Spurious Righteousness (6:1–18)

This passage expands the idea of Christian righteousness as contrasted with the righteousness of the scribes and Pharisees (5:20). Righteousness is illustrated by three basic acts of Jewish piety: almsgiving, prayer, and fasting. In each instance an antithesis is drawn between the spurious piety of display and the genuine piety, which seeks to conceal itself. The ideal of this passage lacks a certain harmony with that of 5:14–16—an inconsistency not so

Book One: The Proclamation of the Reign (3:1—7:29)

much in the text as in the situation: works of piety should not be done for vain display, but they should have the force of good example. If they stem from the proper motive, they will be seen—a city set on a mountain cannot be hidden.

(i) Almsgiving (6:1-4)

1. *righteousness*: In later biblical literature and extrabiblical Jewish writings this becomes the technical term for almsgiving; and the word may have this force here (some mss. indeed read *eleēnosynēn*), although this is not the usual meaning of the word in Mt. The language in which vain display is repudiated is unusually vigorous. 2. *hypocrites*: This word originally meant "actor," and this meaning may be echoed here; the word "to be seen" used in 6:1 is the Gk verb related to the noun "theater." Genuine righteousness even tries to evade itself. To be hailed as a virtuous man is a sufficient reward for those who seek recognition; they obtain what they seek, and that is all they obtain.

(ii) Prayer (6:5-15)

The saying on prayer follows the pattern of the saying on almsgiving. The prayer in public was prayer that was uttered at set times of the day; the devout Jew stopped wherever he was, unless the place was unclean, and recited the proper prayers in a standing position. Moslems also worship in public at prescribed times, and it is regarded as a sign of great devotion to observe this practice. 6. *retire to your room*: In a phrase borrowed from Is 26:20, quoted according to the LXX, the saying recommends that one retire to one's private chamber even to recite the scheduled prayer. Prayer said when one is not being observed is surely prompted by the proper motive. The saying does not refer to public common prayer in the temple or the synagogue.

Verses 7 to 15 interrupt the pattern and are placed here under a loose topical arrangement. The Lord's Prayer in Lk 11:2-4 is given in answer to a request from the disciples for instruction in prayer, and this is no doubt the original context of the prayer in Q. The Lord's Prayer is contrasted in 6:7-8 not with Jewish prayer but with pagan prayer, which is dismissed as "babbling." There may be an allusion to the long and tedious magical formulas in which meaningless epithets are piled up (C. K. Barrett, *NTB* 31-35). The saying is not sympathetic to long prayers, however, of which Judaism of NT times presents numerous examples. The lengthy recital of one's needs is discouraged on the ground that God does not need to be informed of them.

The Lord's Prayer in Lk has a shorter invocation and six petitions against Mt's seven, omitting the third petition in Mt. 9. *Father in heaven*: A common phrase of Mt (5:45; 7:21; 12:50). The first three petitions are really synonymous; they express the desire for the eschatological realization of the reign. *hallowed be your name*: This occurs when it is recognized as holy and confessed to be holy by men. The coming of the reign is the effective actualization of the will of God "on earth as in heaven," where God's supremacy is not questioned. 11. *daily*: The word *epiousios*, traditionally translated "daily," is of uncertain meaning; it does not appear in any Gk literature before the Gospels, and the etymology is uncertain. "Daily" is a very probable rendering; the word seems to designate the bread of the coming day, and the petition is thus related to the sayings against excessive solicitude (6:31–33). However, K. Stendahl has raised the question whether the petition may not refer to the Messianic banquet (*PCB* 778); see comment on 8:11. This also is in harmony with 6:31–33; for the petition is then not directed even to the simple provision of daily basic needs, but to the ultimate realization of the reign in which basic daily needs cease to exist. In this interpretation the fourth petition belongs with the first three. 12. *our debts*: The fifth petition is a prayer for the forgiveness of them. Lk has "sins," an easier word for non-Jewish readers. The condition of forgiveness is that one has forgiven. 13. *lead us not into temptation*: This petition probably does not refer to the daily encounter with evil; Matthew would no doubt agree with Paul that God can give an escape from temptation (1 Cor 10:13). The eschatological tone of the prayer suggests that the temptation meant is the great eschatological test, of which Mt says (24:22) that no one could bear it unless it were abbreviated. *deliver us from evil*: Similarly, the eschatological catastrophe is very probably "the evil" from which the Christian prays to be delivered in the final petition. The ambiguity of "evil" and "the evil one" previously noted (5:37,39) is found here too.

A doxology, "For thine is the kingdom and the power and the glory forever and ever, Amen" is found in many Gk mss: The presence of a similar doxology in the *Didache* (8:2), a work written before AD 100, suggests that the doxology is a very early expansion. It was normal in Judaism to conclude prayers with a formal doxology, and the early Christian communities often followed the Jewish practice. The doxology, however, is not found in

BOOK ONE: THE PROCLAMATION OF THE REIGN (3:1—7:29)

the most reliable mss. It has been used in the Protestant churches; it is sheer accident that it did not appear in the Gk mss that Jerome used in translating the Vg.

Verses 14 and 15 are a commentary on the fifth petition, emphasizing the duty of forgiveness as a condition of receiving forgiveness. The passage is very loosely parallel to Mk 11:25–26. See 5:23–26; 18:35.

(iii) Fasting (6:16–18)

16. *when you fast*: In the early books of the OT, fasting appears as a token of mourning or of repentance. No fast is prescribed in the Law except the fast of the Day of Atonement (Lv 16:29; 23:27; Nm 29:7). A fast meant abstinence from food for the entire day from sunrise to sunset. Fasting twice a week was regarded in NT times as a sign of devotion. *they disfigure their faces*: The disfigurement was a part of the ritual of grief or mourning in the ancient world; "sackcloth and ashes" were put on to make the person unsightly. These are rejected as mere external display. The disciple who fasts should wash and anoint himself; washing and anointing were preparations for a banquet, not signs of grief and affliction (see 9:14–15).

(e) Sayings (6:19–34)

This collection of sayings, which are found in scattered contexts in Lk, have as a common theme singleness of purpose. The disciple should attend exclusively to the service of God and should not permit himself to be distracted from this concentration even by what men think are legitimate cares. The paradoxical tone of the sermon is maintained in these sayings.

(i) True treasure (6:19–21)

The Palestinian archaeologist sometimes finds hoards of coins in the remains of ancient houses. More frequently he finds only traces of such hoards. The ancient peasant or laborer had very little opportunity to use hard money; and when it came into his hands, his instinct was to bury it rather than spend it. He was especially moved to hide his little store of coins at times of political disturbance: and there was always the danger of thieves or robbers (6:19). The saying tells the disciples that no lasting treasure can be stored on earth. The stores of the peasant often included costly garments, which were saved for special occasions. These will be eaten by moths. "Rust" is literally "eating," any type of corrosion. 20. *dig through and steal:* This could be done by thieves in a house of mud bricks, no longer the prevalent building material in modern Palestine, where stone is now commonly used. There are other references to mud-brick houses; see 7:26–27. *treasure in heaven:* This metaphor is in the same line with the "wages" mentioned in the preceding examples of true righteousness (6:1,4,6). Only righteousness achieves anything of lasting value; and what a man thinks has lasting value determines where his intentions and interests lie.

(ii) The single eye (6:22–23)

22. *the eye is the lamp of the body:* In a naïve physiological conception the eye is the aperture through which light is admitted. The eye should be simple, which means healthy; the Hebr or Aram background is not certain, but this is the most probable meaning of the word. The healthy eye illuminates the whole inner man. The "evil," or wicked, eye is here the diseased eye; if the very principle of light is darkened, then the whole inner man is in total darkness. The force of the metaphor is somewhat obscure both in Mt and in Lk. The "evil eye" is usually envy; and the original saying seems to have been directed against this vice. By inserting it in the present context Mt has turned it to an image of simplicity of intention; this is the clarity of vision by which one seeks true treasure and serves only one master.

(iii) Two masters (6:24)

This saying continues the common theme. The disciple cannot have a divided loyalty. *Mammon:* personified in opposition to God, it is found in the Talmud to designate not only money, but possessions in general. Taken together with 6:19–21 and the following passage, the radical character of the teaching of Jesus on wealth and ownership begins to emerge. Material possessions are a false god that demands exclusive loyalty, as God demands it. The claims of material possessions must be totally repudiated.

Book One: The Proclamation of the Reign (3:1—7:29)

(iv) Solicitude (6:25-34)

The radical teaching of Jesus on possessions is expanded and emphasized. *worry:* "Anxious care" is not to be admitted; it may be worth noting that the word means more than simple thought or planning. Jesus refers to the kind of worry that leads to a divided loyalty and ultimately to an exclusive concentration on possessions. He speaks of the basic needs of food and clothing—the person is more important and deserves more attention than the external goods that sustain him. The example of the birds is proposed as the proper attitude toward food. T. H. Robinson has remarked that this example does not excuse one from earning his food; few men, he says, work as hard for their living as the average sparrow. The audience to which these sayings were addressed was largely composed of peasants and laborers, and Jesus says nothing here or elsewhere that invites them to abandon their life of incessant grinding toil. It is not indolence he recommends (see 2 Thes 3:10). What is recommended is that one's anxiety should not exceed the labor that is required to secure subsistence. It is not the use of the necessities of life that is discouraged, but the accumulation of goods. Accumulation of goods does not prolong the life of the owner as much as a cubit (about 18–20 in.). The spatial and temporal metaphors are mixed in this figure.

25. *what you shall put on:* For the proper attitude toward clothing, Jesus alludes to the wild flowers, which bloom in profusion on Palestinian hills. These hills are a dull brown color most of the year. The example illustrates the observation of nature and the details of daily life that are typical of the Gospels. Yet this display of bright color, which is indeed an impressive sight, lasts only for a few weeks. 29. *Solomon in all his splendor:* The raiment of Solomon, the proverbial example of wealth in the Bible, did not effectively endure much longer. To make the provision of food and clothing one's major concern, an object of anxiety, is to live like the pagans who know no dedication except to the accumulation of the goods of this world. The disciples have a prior dedication, the reign of God; Mt adds "its righteousness" (see 5:20), not found in Lk. If the disciples seek this, God will provide the necessities of life to those who work for them. 34. This verse (not found in Lk) emphasizes more clearly the principle that the disciples should not accumulate goods. By a saying paradoxical to modern ears, saving is called anxious care for the morrow; no doubt this is an instance (similar to the legitimation of what was once called usury) of the adaptation of the Gospels to an economics not the same as that in which the Gospels were written. If saving becomes "accumulation," it is still

27

subject to the words of this passage. *sufficient for the day:* The concluding sentence sounds less like a saying of Jesus than a popular proverb used to illustrate the point at issue.

(f) Collection of Detached Sayings (7:1–27)

The remainder of the sermon has no perceptible unity of theme. Obviously Matthew considered the sayings to be basic. Almost all of them are paralleled in Lk; but only one is paralleled in Mk.

(i) Judging others (7:1–5)

1. *judge not:* The meaning of "judge" is not simply to have an opinion—this can scarcely be avoided; the word means to judge harshly, to condemn, and the form in which the saying appears in Lk (6:37–38) makes this explicit. Mt's briefer statement is probably closer to the original. 2. This saying is found in Mk 4:24 in a different context. It suits Matthew's purpose quite well. Men must judge one another, but they can expect to be called to responsibility for their judgments. By a somewhat popular paradox one who judges others unfairly is apparently threatened with the unfair judgment of God. This is not the intended meaning; harsh judgments will be punished severely, but not unfairly. Lk 6:38 has adapted the saying to a different context; the measure is not the measure of judgment but the measure of generous giving. The name of God is avoided; the threat of judgment is put in the simple passive ("theological" passive, *Gr Bib* § 236). 3. *the beam:* By a hyperbole the "beam" in one's own eye is contrasted with the "splinter" in another's eye. This may be a popular proverb applied to the Gospel. Acute observance of the faults of others combined with complacency with one's own character is the object to many commonplace proverbs in all languages. This is the attitude of "hypocrites" (see comment on 6:2); the saying is clearly directed against the censoriousness of the scribes and Pharisees.

(ii) Pearls before swine (7:6)

This saying has furnished interpreters difficulty; it is not clear what is concealed by the figure. The saying is chiastic. Its original form may have been: "Give not the holy to dogs/lest they tear you;/nor cast your pearls before

Book One: The Proclamation of the Reign (3:1—7:29)

swine/lest they trample them." Whatever the original force of the saying was (another popular proverb?), in Mt it most probably refers to the proclamation and teaching of the Gospel. In this hypothesis the dogs and the swine can scarcely be any but those who in Mt are least hospitable to the Gospel: the scribes and Pharisees. The saying is harsh, but more so to us than it would be in its original utterance; the use of popular proverbs in this fashion was a commonplace of ancient Near Eastern wisdom.

(iii) Prayer and its answer (7:7–11)

7. *ask and it will be given:* Prayer to most people means the prayer of petition, and this is the prayer recommended here. The deliberate repetition of the threefold formula, ask-receive, seek-find, knock-be-opened, is intended to assure the disciples that prayer is heard and to encourage them to present their petitions to God. There is no real opposition between this passage and 6:8,32, where Jesus speaks of the prayer of worried anxiety, which reflects the excessive solicitude of those who utter it. It is possible that the type of nervous care discussed in 6:25–34 can reflect itself in the prayer of the worried person. Prayer should be uttered in the spirit of freedom from worry and in the assurance that it is heard and answered. 9. *if a son asks for bread:* The assurance is illustrated by homely examples from family life; the father will give his children what they ask, and he certainly will not give them something harmful in answer to their requests. The bread is the round loaf that has a strange resemblance to a stone. Mt uses this example instead of the picturesque example of the egg and the scorpion (Lk 11:12); this well-known Palestinian nuisance roughly resembles an egg. 11. *you who are evil:* Fathers, even though they are "evil," take care of their children; this is merely a statement of the human condition. The Father in heaven is not evil, and can be counted on to act like a father.

(iv) The golden rule (7:12)

This verse has parallels both in Judaism and in other ancient literature (Str-B 1, 459–60). The best known is probably the saying attributed to Rabbi Hillel, given in answer to the challenge of a proselyte to explain the whole Law while the proselyte stood on one foot: "That which displeases you do not do to another. This is the whole Law; the rest is commentary." The saying of Hillel is echoed in the last part of Mt's sentence, not found in Lk; but the saying attributed to Hillel cannot be dated. The addition of Mt does not support the claim that the saying is entirely new in Christianity, as indeed it is not. Not too much, it seems, should be made of the fact that the Gospel saying is couched in the affirmative, whereas the parallels are couched in the negative; this distinction seems to be hairsplitting.

(v) The narrow gate (7:13-14)

The saying in Lk is given in answer to the question whether few are saved. The question is not found in Mt, but the saying is no less eschatological. The ms. evidence for 7:13b in the form most frequently quoted, "Wide is the gate and spacious the way," is ample; but the critical text reads, "Wide and spacious is the way." Where Lk says there are few who seek the narrow gate, Mt says there are few who find it; Mt's formula is slightly more rigorous. The saying echoes the rather common teaching of the two spirits and the two ways, found in 1QS 3:20-21; *Didache* 1:1—6:2; *Ep. Barnabae* 18:1—21:9.

(vi) Genuine good works (7:15-20)

Lk (6:43-45) does not contain the warning against false prophets; see 24:11. These do not seem to be "false teachers," but those who claim a new revelation; possibly the saying refers to the Zealot prophets who incited to rebellion against Rome during the period preceding the Jewish War AD 66-70. In any case, the addition of Mt seems to reflect the experience of the Church. 16. *by their fruits:* The true test of prophets or disciples is their life. The comparison of trees and fruits is painfully elaborated. Luke felt the necessity of explaining the comparison (6:45), with the addition of a phrase that makes speech the principal fruit; this is not the real meaning of the original comparison, which refers to deeds. See the recital in Mt 23. 19. This verse is repeated word for word from the preaching of John the Baptist (3:10), where it has a more suitable context.

(vii) Self-deception (7:21-23)

21. *Lord, Lord:* This address, "Lord, Lord," reflects the experience of the primitive Church. It is most likely that the reference to prophecy, exorcism,

Book One: The Proclamation of the Reign (3:1—7:29)

and thaumaturgy also refers to the experience of the primitive Church. Devout invocation of Jesus as Lord and the reception of the charismata of the apostolate do not guarantee that one is a genuine disciple. Paul also says that these gifts are vain without love (1 Cor 13:2). In Mt the test is doing the will of the Father (Lk 6:46, "doing what I tell you"). 22. *on that day:* In the eschatological judgment Jesus will profess that he does not know them. 23. The formula of reprobation is quoted from Ps 6:9; neither Mt nor Lk quotes the LXX exactly. The form of the saying in Lk 13:26-27 ("We have eaten and drunk with you, and you have taught in our streets") points the saying much more directly to the Jews. In Mt the saying is directed at false disciples within the Christian community.

(viii) Hearers and doers (7:24-27)

The words of Jesus are a call and a challenge to action; they are not mere teaching, and understanding them is an insufficient response. The challenge is serious; failure to meet it is followed by catastrophe—"great is the fall." This again is the eschatological catastrophe. 24. *upon the rock:* The comparison of the house builders presupposes Palestinian conditions; Luke, however, was not familiar with these. He describes the digging of a deep foundation (6:48). It is rather striking that Hellenistic buildings in Palestinian sites were built on deeper foundations than earlier buildings; but this was the practice with large houses or public buildings, not with the ordinary dwelling. The flood Luke envisages is the flood of a river. Matthew knows the Palestinian winter rains that run off in sudden large flows of water. These rains not only fill the stream beds (*wadis*) with rapid torrents but erode the slopes of the hills. The soil is swept from beneath a house that is not founded on the bedrock. The house built of mud brick is particularly vulnerable. It is action, not knowledge or profession of belief, that furnishes the secure foundation for the life of the disciple; and the love without which Paul says charismata are vain is action, not mere profession of belief.

(g) Concluding Formula (7:28-29)

Each of the major discourses of Mt is concluded by a similar formula. The result of his teaching, in a phrase taken from Mk (1:22), is astonishment. The astonishment is not attributed to the content of the teaching, but to the manner in which it was proposed: Jesus teaches with authority unlike that of the scribes. The authority of the scribes was based on tradition: The scribe was careful to repeat the traditional teaching and to show that his own commentary rose from the tradition and was in harmony with it. The first part of the sermon [→ Chapter 2: (B) Discourse: (c) The Law and the Gospel: (i)-(vi)] is a deliberate and explicit departure from tradition. Jesus taught not like a scribe but like a prophet, although the word is not used. The Gk word *exousia* translated "authority" means "authority by commission." Jesus has a commission from the Father to teach—a commission the scribes do not have. He manifests this commission clearly, and the people are astonished.

General Remarks

The Sermon on the Mount is not "the New Law"; this phrase is nowhere applied to the sermon, and the sermon is not couched either in the form of the Law or in the form of rabbinical teaching. It is very probably a form of Christian teaching (*didachē*), the instruction given to those who had believed in the proclamation (*kerygma*) and received baptism. It was formed by a more or less systematic collection and arrangement of remembered sayings of Jesus, adapted and clarified where necessary for the group that was being instructed.

The sermon is not a complete code of Christian ethics. There are many directions for Christian morality in the NT that are not found in the sermon. Indeed no single passage of the NT contains a complete and systematic code of conduct. The Christian moral revolution consisted in a reorientation of values. This can be expressed in a few simple phrases, most of which can be summed up as directions to love. Other moral directions are applications of the principle of love. The sermon is a statement of those principles "Matthew" or his sources considered basic enough to be collected and placed in the significant position of introducing the account of the words and deeds of Jesus.

(Dupont, J., *Les béatitudes* [new ed. ; Bruges, 1958]. Hunter, A. M., "The Meaning of the Sermon on the Mount," *ExpT* 63 [1951–52] 176–79. Jeremias, J., *The Sermon on the Mount* [Facet, Bibl. ser., 2; Phila., 1963], McArthur, K. H., *Understanding the Sermon on the Mount* [N.Y., 1960]. Schnackenburg, R., *The Moral Teaching of the NT* [N.Y., 1965]. Windisch, H., *The Meaning of the Sermon on the Mount* [Phila., 1951].)

Chapter 3

Book Two
Ministry in Galilee (8:1—11:1)

(A) Narrative Section: Cycle of Ten Miracles (8:1—9:34)

THIS SECTION HAS AS its basic content ten miracles, most of which are found in Mk. The order of Mk, however, is revised. Mk's "Day in Capernaum" has nearly disappeared as such, and materials that follow the call of the apostles in Mk have been placed before it by Mt. The events are arranged to form an introduction to the discourse on the apostolic mission, which concludes Book Two.

(a) The Healing of a Leper (8:1–4)

This passage illustrates how Mt normally abbreviates the narratives of Mk (see 1:40–45) by the omission of picturesque details. In Mt the incident takes place in a location between the "mountain" of the sermon and Capernaum; in Mk and Lk it is placed somewhere in Galilee. Mt, because the incident follows the sermon, makes mention of a crowd with Jesus. 2. *leper:* Leprosy is loosely used throughout the Bible for unspecified skin diseases (cf. Lv 13), which were as common in the Near East of NT times as they are today. The type of disease is not pertinent to the miraculous character of the cure; eczema seems no easier to heal by a touch than leprosy. 3. *I will; be made clean:* All three Gospels retain the formula in which the words of Jesus echo the petition of the sick man; faith is not mentioned in the narrative, but the brevity of the petition and the instant echo of the answer illustrate the faith of the sick man and the healing power of Jesus. Both Mt and Lk omit the words that express the emotional reaction of Jesus: "feeling compassion" (Mk 1:41) and "angered" (1:43). Indeed Mk 1:43 must have been as unintelligible to Matthew and Luke as it is to modern readers; the verse surely reflects the constructive work of Mark, and the original form of the story must have represented the leprosy as the work of a demon. It is the demon and not the sufferer who is the object of the anger of Jesus and who is expelled in Mk. The precept of silence is important in Mk; it is a part of that pattern called "the Messianic Secret." Mt and Lk retain the precept, even though the pattern of the secret is not an essential part of their Gospels. Mt consequently omits Mk's notice that the secret was not kept. 4. *show yourself to the priest*: The appearance of the leper before the priest with an offering to certify his cure is prescribed in Lv 14:2-9.

(b) The Slave of the Centurion (8:5-13)

In contrast to the preceding incident, this passage illustrates the "saying-story" as opposed to the "miracle story." In the healing of the leper, the miracle itself is the point of the story. In the story of the centurion, the miracle is the occasion by which the faith of the Gentile centurion is manifested; and his faith in turn is the occasion of the saying of Jesus (8:10-12). The story is not found in Mk, and the variations between Mt and Lk are such as to raise some doubt whether the story was found in Q. These doubts do not appear to be well founded; a comparison of Mt and Lk shows that Matthew uses his customary technique of abbreviating narratives.

The scene is Capernaum. 5. *a centurion*: The petitioner is an officer of the Roman legions whose command was normally 100 men (Lat *centum*, 100); but the number could be more or less. These officers, who corresponded somewhat to our noncommissioned officers, were usually in charge of small local posts and garrisons. It is interesting to note that every one of these officers who appears in the NT is an honest and kindly man. The sick person is called "slave" (*doulos*) by Lk, a "boy" (*pais*) by Mt; but *pais* was a common Gk designation of a young slave. The disease cannot be identified; paralysis means the loss of the use of the limbs, and here it is accompanied with great pain; this detail is not found in Lk. 7. This verse is understood by many interpreters as a question: "Shall I come and heal

Book Two: Ministry in Galilee (8:1—11:1)

him?" Normally a Jew would not enter the house of a Gentile; he would incur ritual uncleanness. Mt makes the centurion the petitioner; Lk has the centurion send Jews as his emissaries and intercessors, and the centurion does not appear until Jesus is on his way to the house. This is more probably an omission by Mt rather than an expansion of Lk. The omission unfortunately leaves out a pleasing detail of excellent relations between a Gentile and the Jewish community. The omission, however, takes no more credit from one party than from the other; and it is economical rather than tendentious. 8. The climactic line in both versions is the centurion's belief that Jesus need only speak; a visit and personal contact are unnecessary. 9. *a man under authority*: He illustrates from his own position. He, a military officer of lower rank, gets instant obedience and execution from men under him; if military discipline can effect things by a word, Jesus is surely no less "under authority." 10. The answer of Jesus is the first saying in Mt that contrasts the unbelief of the Jews with the faith of the uninstructed Gentile. Actually at this point in Mt's narrative the unbelief of the Jews has not yet appeared; in Mt's version even the request of the Jews that Jesus should come to the house to heal the slave (Lk 5:3) is omitted. In Lk, likewise, the faith of the centurion seems to grow from the initial request to the point where he intercepts Jesus.

11–12. This saying is found in Lk (13:28–30) in a different and entirely eschatological context, which is probably its original situation. "The sons of the kingdom" are simply "you" in Lk. The Gentiles will be admitted with the true Israelites to the Messianic banquet. This theme is based on Is 25:6–8; it conceives the Messianic deliverance as admission to a festive dinner that God prepares. The Messianic banquet is found in apocalyptic literature and in the Qumran writings and is echoed frequently in the NT. It is a part of the idea of the Eucharist (see 26:29). 12b. An eschatological commonplace in Mt (13:42,50; 22:13; 24:51; 25:30).

The theme of the story is faith—the kind of faith that sets no conditions. The choice of a Gentile to illustrate this faith the first time the idea is raised in the Gospel is certainly deliberate; it sets a tone Mt maintains in the rest of the book: The faith of the Gentiles gives them the title of the true Israel which the Jews have forfeited by unbelief in the Messiah.

No doubt Jn 4:46–52 is a variant of the same story, but it is so profoundly modified that a common source cannot be traced with certainty.

(c) Peter's Mother-in-law (8:14–15)

This is another instance of Matthew's economy with Mk's material (Mk 1:29–31). He omits all names except the name of Peter, the intercession of the family, and picturesque details in the cure itself. Commentators believe the change from "she served them" to "she served him" is significant; Jesus is more than one of a group. This episode and 1 Cor 9:5 show that Peter was married.

(d) Healings and Exorcisms (8:16–17)

The evening is the evening of Mk's "Day in Capernaum," of which Mt has preserved only this passage and the preceding incident (Mk 1:32–34). The Gospels distinguish between those "possessed by demons" and the "ill"; not every illness was regarded as the work of a demon. It is doubtful that Mark meant to say that they brought all the ill and Jesus cured some; but Matthew in any case alters Mk to say that Jesus healed "all." 16. *by a word*: A Matthaean addition emphasizing the easy exercise of power. Allusion to the Messianic secret (see comment on 8:4) is omitted, but a fulfillment quotation from Is 53:4 (see comment on 1:24) is added. The text is quoted not according to the LXX but according to the MT; and the meaning is altered by a wordplay. The passage of Is refers to the vicarious suffering of the Servant of the Lord, who takes upon himself the illnesses and the stripes of others. Mt interprets the words "take" and "carry" as take away, which Jesus does by healing.

(e) Discipleship and Renunciation (8:18–22)

18. This connecting verse is peculiar to Mt, which has its own arrangement. Jesus commands a voyage to the eastern shore of the Sea of Galilee, opposite Capernaum, in order to escape the crowds. Actually the chief reason for the command in Mt is to provide an occasion to insert the stories of the calming of the storm and the demoniacs of Gadara. The two sayings about discipleship are placed in Lk at the beginning of the Journey Narrative; they had no original context in Q. Both the speakers are disciples. Matthew presupposes the formation of a group of intimate associates who accompanied Jesus, although he has not yet described the formation of such a group except in the story of the call (4:18–22). 19. *a scribe*: The first speaker

BOOK TWO: MINISTRY IN GALILEE (8:1—11:1)

belongs to a group usually represented as hostile to Jesus, yet there were scribes among the members of the primitive Christian community. His words are not meant to be insincere; they are the occasion for the statement of Jesus that those who follow him must be prepared to have no home, as he has none. There are no other clear references to the fact that Jesus was technically a vagrant, but no home is ever mentioned. The form of expression is possibly based on a popular proverb. 20. *Son of Man:* This title, used frequently of Jesus, appears for the first time here in Mt. 21. *another of his disciples:* The second disciple wishes to bury his father. This does not mean that his father had died (burial normally occurred on the day of death), but that the disciple wished to await his father's death so that he might provide for him. But renunciation of family ties is one of the conditions of discipleship; one cannot wait until all family connections are satisfied, or one would never be able to follow the call. The time is now (see 10:37).

(f) The Tempest at Sea (8:23–27)

Here Matthew has compressed the narrative less than usual, and his changes are significant. For Mk's "whirlwind" has become a *seismos*, "earthquake," a cosmic disturbance. In Mk (4:35–41) the boat is shipping water, in Mt it is nearly covered by the waves. In Mk the cry of the disciples is not a petition for help—how could they expect to be saved from a storm? In Mt it is a prayer for deliverance addressed to Jesus, the *Kyrios*; and this change is not altogether consistent with the rebuke in which they are called "you of little faith." 24. *a great storm:* The *seismos* (above). Modern observers have noticed that the Sea of Galilee, a small body of water almost entirely surrounded by hills, is often subject to sudden storms because of currents of air of variant temperatures that roll down the slopes. The storms abate as suddenly as they arise. It seems unlikely that the disciples, who had lived on the Sea of Galilee all their lives, did not know this. The story opens another aspect of the mystery of Jesus: his mastery over nature, which is more awesome than his mastery over disease and demons. The disciples simply ask who he is; the rest of the Gospel is taken up with the revelation of the answer to the question. 27. *the men:* This word seems to admit others than the disciples as witnesses of the miracle, although he has left no room for others in the preceding narrative; Mk, however, notes that the boat was accompanied by other boats (4:36).

(g) The Demoniacs of Gadara (8:28–34)

Mt designates the location of the story more correctly than Mk or Lk. The Hellenistic city of Gadara lay nearer to the Sea of Galilee than the Hellenistic city of Gerasa. The variant reading Gergesenes comes from an erudite conjecture of Origen. The story is told in Mk with full and circumstantial details. It has obvious folkloristic traits, is vivid, and moves rapidly. Even Matthew's condensation retains more length than his miracle stories usually have; but he has omitted most of Mk's details. 28. *two demoniacs*: Instead of Mk's one (5:2–5); Mt omits Mk's description of the ferocity of the demoniac. In the ancient world, Jewish and Gentile, ailments which exhibited some unusually repulsive feature or for which there was no explanation were often attributed to demons. It is rarely possible to define the ailment that is explained in this way; mental illness, of course, was more obviously explained by demonic possession than was physical disease. The important feature of this and other exorcisms performed by Jesus is not whether he accepted the common belief or spoke in terms of the common belief; those who formed the Gospel traditions could not have represented him as speaking in terms other than those familiar to them. The important fact is that the exorcisms show that Jesus liberates men from the fear of demons; demons have no real power and are instantly subdued by a word from him. The power of God overcomes any other power. The significance of exorcism is not that the Christian should or should not believe in demons and their power, but that the Christian should treat demonic power as nonexistent. There is only one power with which men must reckon, and that is the power of God. 29. *what have you to do with us*: Lit., "what to us and to you?" The phrase expresses dissociation; it denies both community of interest and grounds for hostility and is effectively a dismissal. But the demons recognize Jesus. *Son of God*: The title has rather full implications here. The dark powers of the world of spirits know with whom they have to contend before he is recognized by men. *before the time*: The *kairos* is the appointed time for the eschatological consummation, when God will destroy every hostile power (1 Cor 15:24–25). 31. *the demons begged him*: The request of the demons to be sent into the herd of pigs is not mere mischievousness; the pig, the most unclean of all animals, is the suitable place for a demon. The presence of the herd shows that the episode occurs in Gentile territory. 32. *rushed . . . into the sea*: The rush of the pigs into the sea may seem a bit unfair to their owners; but in Jewish thought the unclean pig was good for absolutely nothing at all, and no one could incur a loss when a herd of pigs perished. Does the narrative mean that the demons perished? This seems to be the implication. The demons were driven from men into pigs, but even the pigs reject them; demons have no place in a world in which the saving power of God has entered in Jesus Christ.

Mt also omits most of the details of the recovery of the demoniacs. 34. *they begged him to leave their neighborhood*: Mk does not exhibit in the story any of the remarkable faith shown by such Gentiles as the centurion. One who has power over demons is a dangerous person and may even himself be a demon of higher power; this is the point of the accusation of the Pharisees (12:24). The story is an instance of the failure of a wonder to inspire faith, and the Gospels make no comment on the reasons. Mt omits the request of the man to follow Jesus, and the commission Jesus gives him to proclaim the wonder (Mk 5:18–19).

(h) Healing and Forgiveness of Sins (9:1–8)

This passage is a "controversy-story" in which the miracle is the resolution of a controversy. The progress of Mt's arrangement is obvious: from disease to nature to demonic possession to the power to forgive sins, the climactic exhibition of a power that belongs to God alone (Mk 2:7), a phrase Mt strangely omits. 1. *his own city*: The scene is Capernaum, to which Jesus returns from the eastern shore of the Sea of Galilee. Mt calls Capernaum "his own city" (9:1), which does not indicate that Jesus had a house there (see 8:20); it was the city to which he returned during the Galilean ministry. Matthew abbreviates Mk even in the dialogue, which is the central part of the story; he omits the presence of crowds and the almost bizarre detail of the digging of a hole in the roof in order to get the paralytic into the room. 2. *their faith*: The appearance of the sick man and his manifest faith elicit not a cure but a declaration of forgiveness of sins, which is not the expected response. Yet it is fully in harmony with the evangelical understanding of miracles. The miracle is worked in response to the faith of the petitioner; and faith in Jesus is already an implicit confession of sin and of repentance. The afflictions of the human condition are the consequences of sin, and forgiveness of sins removes the root of evil. The miracle is far more than a mere wonder; it is at once a symbol and a token of the saving process, which is initiated in Jesus. This conception of miracle escapes the scribes, who see in the words of Jesus an assertion of divine prerogatives. Jesus does not withdraw from his position but challenges them to an ordeal. 5. *which is easier:* To say that sins are forgiven, which cannot be tested by observation, or to bid the sick man rise and walk. The effect of the healing power shows that the power that saves from sin is present and active. Unless sin is cured, there is no genuine remedy for human ills. This is the point of Mt's version of the concluding verse; it is the fullness of the saving power—not the mere power of thaumaturgy—that causes men to glorify God.

(i) The Call of Matthew (9:9–13)

This is a "controversy-story" that ends in a saying; the vocation of Matthew is the occasion of the controversy. The tax collector is named Levi in Mk 2:14; Lk 5:27,29, and only in these passages; the name Matthew appears here and in all the lists of the Twelve. The tax collectors are known in the Gospels as a typical class of moral reprobates, sometimes paired with sinners (as in 9:10–11). The Roman taxes were collected by tax farmers, who bid for the right to collect taxes and then extorted them to the limit. They were therefore not only considered oppressors; they were traitors to their own people because they collaborated with the foreign imperial power.

If Matthew is the author of the First Gospel, then this passage would be autobiographical. In this hypothesis, it is strange that this passage shows exactly the same kind of dependence on Mk and the same type of revision found elsewhere. The revisions are actually slight, consisting of a few omissions and the addition of 9:13. Matthew follows the call with the same immediacy that is seen in the call of the fishermen (4:18–22); the promptness of Matthew's response is more remarkable because he is such an unlikely subject. 10. His second response is a gesture of hospitality; he invites Jesus to a farewell dinner with his friends, "tax collectors and sinners." The "sinners" are nonobservant Jews. 11. *why does your teacher eat . . . :* Pharisaic Judaism held strictly to the principle of avoiding contact with Gentiles and Jews who did not observe the Law; these were the social outcasts of the community, and no rabbi could afford to consort with such. The remark may express surprise as much as hostility; but the snobbish attitude that underlies the remark elicits a sharp response from Jesus. 12. *need no physician:* Jesus' saying is cast in a proverbial form, and in Mt it is strengthened by the quotation of Hos 6:6 (LXX). The quotation places human relations above cultic worship, and of course above mere observance of an external manner of life. The quotation and the saying express the compassion of Jesus for sinners, to whom his mission is directed, but it also strikes at

Book Two: Ministry in Galilee (8:1—11:1)

the self-righteousness of the Pharisees. Those who do not recognize their illness will not summon the physician nor receive him; they are beyond healing. No one can approach Jesus unless he confesses that he is a sinner. The position of this story after the story of the healing of the paralytic is extremely apt in the Gospels. The faith that heals demands repentance.

(j) Fasting (9:14-17)

In Mt the question is asked by the disciples of John; in Mk and Lk the questioners are not identified. Fasting was a recognized Jewish observance [→ Chapter 2: (B) Discourse: (d) Genuine and Spurious Righteousness: (i) Almsgiving] that was not practiced by Jesus and his disciples. 15. *can wedding guests mourn*: The question is answered by a saying; possibly the form of the saying is influenced by the fact that fasting was observed in the primitive community. The saying affirms that the sojourn of Jesus with his disciples is considered a time of joy when fasting (or other symbols of grief or mourning) is out of place. Jesus does not reject fasting as such, but asserts the liberty of fasting when it is suitable; he obviously does not regard the Pharisaic customs as obligatory. The comparison of the messianic advent to a wedding festival is found also in 22:1-14; 25:1-13; Ap 19:7-8; these passages, however, are explicitly eschatological. The joy of the eschatological festival is not limited to the end time; it begins with the coming of him who is the bridegroom.

16-17. These sayings have no obvious connection with the preceding, although most commentators seek to establish a relation. The metaphorical language somewhat disguises the radical content of the sayings. The incompatibility of old and new is illustrated with the homely figures of patching with new cloth an old fabric and pouring new wine into used wineskins. The meaning of the figures is that the Gospel is incompatible with the Law. The order Jesus initiates is not a patchwork of elements derived from Judaism and pronouncements of Jesus. It is as new as was the revelation of the Torah through Moses. The statement is as emphatic as anything we read in Paul, although it is in metaphorical language. The novelty of the Gospel should not be overstated, nor is it overstated here; the declaration means that Judaism is not to determine the form the Gospel takes. Whatever value elements of Judaism have in the new order they have from the new order, and not from themselves. Jesus is the supreme interpreter of the Law and the Prophets.

(k) The Ruler's Daughter (9:18–26)

The account of Mk is sharply abbreviated in Mt; and here it is easier to trace the theological basis of the abbreviation. The transitional phrase in Mt connects this incident with the sayings; in Mk the miracle follows the return of Jesus from the territory of Gerasa. 18. *a ruler:* In Mk and Lk the more precise title of synagogue officer appears. In Mt the petition is for a resurrection from the dead; in Mk it is a petition for a cure. The large crowd of Mk does not appear here; this harmonizes with the omission of Mk 5:31–32.

The inserted story of the woman with a hemorrhage (9:20–22) is even more curtailed. The conception of the miraculous power of Jesus is profoundly modified by the omission of Mk 5:29–33. In Mk the power is conceived as a kind of invisible but palpable substance that flows from Jesus by contact, and is effective even when he is touched without his knowledge. But Mt does not conceive power as an emanation; it is operative at the word of Jesus, and the woman is cured not by touching his garment but by his word. Of Mk's narrative Mt preserves the faith that is manifested in her assurance that a touch of Jesus' garment is sufficient to effect a cure. The observant Jew wore a tassel at each of the four corners of his cloak; it was the tassel, not the "fringe," the woman touched.

Mt represents the child as already dead, and the element of suspense becomes superfluous (cf. Mk 5:23,35–36). The musicians and the crowd in the house were professional mourners. 23. *the girl is not dead:* The sleep from which Jesus awakens is death. The raising itself is reduced by Mt to the bare essentials, and the allusion to "the Messianic Secret" (Mk 5:43) is, like most such allusions in Mk, omitted. The rewriting of the story in Mt heightens the wonder of the incident. Where Mk has a healing story, Mt has a resurrection story. This freedom, which to the modern reader may seem unwarranted, rises from the Gospel conception of the miracles. They are, as we have seen, the response of the power of Jesus to faith; and the release of the power corresponds in intensity to the intensity of the faith. The comparison of Mt with Mk here is a good illustration of the type of development that the stories of the deeds of Jesus experienced in the traditions of the primitive Church.

The structure of this part of Mt also may be related to the theological development of the miracle. The three miracles related in this context touch death, blindness, and the loss of speech and hearing. The intention to present a comprehensive summary of the saving power of Jesus is apparent.

BOOK TWO: MINISTRY IN GALILEE (8:1—11:1)

(l) Two Blind Men (9:27-31)

This episode is a doublet of the healing of two blind men at Jericho (see comment on 20:29-34). 27. *Son of David:* This title occurs in both accounts; this was a popular Messianic title, for the king Messiah was a descendant of David and a new David. This version of the incident is expanded by an explicit demand for faith. 30-31. An allusion to "the Messianic Secret," rare in Mt. The reason for the duplication of the incident here is no doubt the threefold classification of the miracles [→ Chapter 3: (A) Narrative Section: (k) The Ruler's Daughter].

(m) A Dumb Man (9:32-34)

In spite of some variations in detail, this passage appears to be an abbreviated doublet of 12:22-24. 34. *the prince of the demons:* The charge of the Pharisees that Jesus was in league with Beelzebul is the occasion of a long controversy in 12:25-37. The reason for the duplication is the same as that given for the preceding passage.

(B) Discourse: The Missionary Sermon (9:35—11:1)

This discourse addressed to the Twelve closes Book Two. It is, like the Sermon on the Mount, a Matthaean construction. Most of the material comes from Q, and some of it is an expansion of Mk. The missionary discourse itself ends at 10:16; the remainder, which is not separated from the missionary discourse, contains sayings on discipleship that are suitable to the context of missionary endeavor. The first of Mt's great discourses was the proclamation of the reign; the second is the first step in the foundation of the Church. In this discourse Jesus admits others to share both his mission and his powers, and he commissions them to proclaim on a scale wider than he could reach personally.

(a) The Sending of the Twelve (9:35—10:4)

The passage opens with a summary of the itinerant preaching of Jesus in Galilee, which is partly repeated from 4:23; the introduction is thus similar to the introduction of the Sermon on the Mount. The new element is the compassion Jesus feels for the multitudes. 36. They are "harassed," "bothered"; this somewhat vulgar Gk word is an excellent term to describe the thousand petty persecutions and annoyances to which the poor are subject. *like sheep without a shepherd:* Cf. 1 Kgs 22:17; the quotation is not from the LXX. The line very probably refers to the *'am hā'āreṣ*, "the people of the land," a contemptuous term used by Pharisees to designate the poor and ignorant who did not know the Law well enough to observe it (Jn 7:49), and often could not afford to observe it. The verse is taken from Mk 6:34, where it precedes the multiplication of the loaves. The compassion that Jesus feels for the hungry in Mk is transferred to the spiritually unenlightened in Mt. 37. *the harvest is plentiful:* This is paralleled in Lk 10:2–3 in the discourse to the 72 disciples. The missionary work of the disciples is also compared to a harvest in Jn 4:35–38 in different terms.

10:1. Mt (with Lk) expands the conferring of power in Mk 6:7 by the addition of the power of healing diseases. This makes explicit what is implicit in Mk; for afflictions are the work of evil spirits, but the attribution to evil spirits is expressed in certain outstanding cases of damage, particularly when the mind is afflicted (see 8:28–34). The designation of the spirits as "unclean" comes from Mk. Although the word usually means immorality associated with sexual experience, this is probably not meant here; the word appears to be synonymous with "evil."

The list of the Twelve has the same names as Mk 3:16–19 with some changes. Peter is singled out as "first" (see comment on 16:13–20). The Twelve are arranged in pairs, with the two sets of brothers mentioned first; this may reflect Mk 6:7, in which the Twelve are sent out in pairs. To the name Matthew is added "the tax collector." The nickname of Boanerges for the sons of Zebedee is omitted. 4. *Cananaean:* Simon's appellative is not the gentilic name of the pre-Israelite people of Palestine, but a Gk transcription of the Aram *qan'ānā(y)*, "Zealot," a member of the radical anti-Roman revolutionary party. Simon had no doubt abandoned this allegiance. *Iscariot.* The Twelve are called "apostles" only here in Mt. No appointment of the Twelve is related by Mt other than this; both Mk and Lk mention the election of the Twelve.

(b) The Discourse Proper (10:5–16)

Verses 5–8 are peculiar to Mt, except for the commissions to proclaim the reign (10:7), where the same words are used that appear in the proclamation of John the Baptist (3:2) and Jesus (4:17). 6. *to the lost sheep of the house*

Book Two: Ministry in Galilee (8:1—11:1)

of Israel: Mt limits the mission of the Twelve to Israel; a similar limitation of the mission of Jesus himself is found in 15:24, also peculiar to Mt. The mission to the Gentiles was as much a fact when Mt was written as it was when Mk and Lk were written, and Mt certainly accepts the mission to the Gentiles. The words are obviously not understood as a precept of Jesus, which the apostolic Church did not follow. They reflect the historical fact, assured in all the Gospels, that the mission of Jesus himself was limited to Jews. More important, they express the principle, not stated so clearly in Mk and Lk, that the Jews had a prior call and a peculiar responsibility. The Jews rejected this call, and the implication is that they lost thereby a peculiar place in the reign. Lk has a similar statement (Acts 13:46–47). These passages suggest that the awareness that there was a mission to the Gentiles developed by stages in the apostolic community; the various NT writings represent different stages. The ideal was that Judaism, transformed by faith in its Messiah, should be the agent of the proclamation to the Gentiles. 8. *heal the sick:* This is a communication of the powers of healing and exorcism to the Twelve. *freely you have received, freely give:* Jesus' saying is illustrated in vv. 9–12, and it was clearly the understanding of the apostolic Church that the gospel was not sold nor were its apostles paid. Several rabbinical sayings preserved in the Talmud warn the rabbi that he must not accept a fee for instruction in the Law; the scribe should have a trade by which he could support himself (Str-B 1, 561–64). It was a point of honor with Paul that he did not even avail himself of the privilege stated here (10:10b; see 1 Cor 9:12). This passage is a more urgent and practical expansion of the discourse about care in the Sermon on the Mount (6:25–34). The prohibition is rigorous in all three Gospels, but there are some variations in detail. Mk has, "Take nothing," Lk has "Take no money," Mt specifies still further "Neither gold nor silver, nor bronze," the metals from which coins were minted. Even the place where coins were usually carried is mentioned, that is, in the girdle. 10. *no bag:* The purse or bag was used to hold food; the ancient traveler, if he was poor, traveled with not much more than the Twelve are permitted here. Mk rather practically allows a staff and sandals; the exclusion of these two articles in Mt and Lk is no doubt an ideal heightening of the poverty of the missionary. *nor two tunics:* To carry a change of linen was a luxury in the ancient world. None of these material things will be needed, for the Twelve will have their needs provided by those to whom they proclaim. 11. *stay with him:* It is not supposed that this provision is the minimum that a hospitable person would offer to any traveler, even to a stranger. This is the food given to the laborer for his labor. Even in the forced labor of the ancient world the laborer received either a small wage or a portion of food for himself and his family for the day. The Twelve are assured this type of support. Paul quotes a saying of Jesus not found in the Gospels (1 Cor 9:14) that makes the proclamation the sole support of the missionaries. It is assumed that they will be unable to support themselves by any other employment. Although Paul did support himself at Corinth, this seems to have been an exception in his own practice. *worthy person:* The adj. "worthy" occurs with unusual frequency in this chapter. "Worth" is shown first by offering hospitality to the missionaries, and secondly by faith in the gospel. 13. *let your peace come upon it:* The blessing to come upon the worthy house was expressed in the usual greeting, "Peace to you"; Lk makes the greeting explicit by quoting the formula. "Peace" is not an adequate translation; the greeting is a wish that all may be well with the person greeted. It is represented as a dynamic word which is sent out by the speaker, and which returns to him if it is unable to fulfill its meaning. *if it is not worthy:* Those who refuse to give hospitality and to listen to the proclamation are to be left; the symbolic action of shaking the dust from the feet expresses complete dissociation. 15. The unbelievers are to be left to the judgment of God; the judgment of Sodom and Gomorrah, which in the OT is the proverbial example of the wrath of God (Gn 19:4), is less severe than the judgment for unbelief. This last expression of condemnation comes from Q. 16. Mt alone has the proverbial saying about the sheep among wolves, the prudence of the serpent, and the simplicity of the dove. Such animal proverbs are found among all peoples, and they appear in the wisdom of the OT. It is a commonplace of wisdom that man combines in himself the paradoxical features of different animals. "Prudent" means that one is thoughtful and perceptive; the serpent always knows where it is going and what it is doing. "Simple" means innocent of malice; the prudence of the missionaries is not the crafty shrewdness of those who are alert to do harm to others. The missionaries are defenseless; this is expanded in the discourse that follows.

(c) Sayings on Discipleship (10:17—11:1)

The rest of this chapter contains a grouping of sayings of Jesus suitable to the missionary endeavor; these sayings have been appended to extend the discourse.

Book Two: Ministry in Galilee (8:1—11:1)

(i) Persecution of the disciples (10:17-25)

This passage reflects the experience of the primitive Church; it alludes to persecution both by Jews (17) and by Gentiles (18). These verses are a fuller form of Mk 13:9, summarized in 24:9; see Lk 21:12-18. **17.** *councils*: The plural refers both to the great council of Jerusalem of 72 members, which heard the case of Jesus and examined the apostles (Acts 3-5), and to local councils. The Talmud prescribes that in a community that numbers as many as 120 there should be a local council of 23 members. **28.** *governors*: A generic name for Roman provincial officers. *kings*: This refers to such satellite rulers as Herod Antipas and Herod Agrippa. The punishment of flogging was suffered by Paul (2 Cor 11:24); it was limited to 40 stripes, always diminished by one to protect the Law. **20.** The assistance of the Spirit is promised the disciples when they have to bear witness for Jesus (see Mk 13:11; Jn 14:26; Lk 21:14-15; 12:11-12). Such charismatic witness is related in Acts 4:8; 13:9. **21.** The gospel will be a cause of division in families; this seems to refer primarily to Jewish families. The hatred of all men comes from Mk 13:13; Mt uses the line again in 24:9. The line is a strange inversion of the charge of *odium generis humani*, "hatred of the human race," which Roman writers laid against Christians. **22.** *he who endures to the end*: Sustains persecution even to death. *will be saved*: Here "being saved" has not the usual meaning of escaping with one's life, but of assuring one's eschatological salvation. **23.** *flee to the next town*: The disciples are not to sacrifice themselves rashly; the proclamation of the gospel is their primary task, and if they are prevented from proclaiming the gospel in one place they should move on to another. **23b.** *before the Son of Man comes*: This verse is an ancient exegetical puzzle. If it means that the parousia is expected before the disciples even begin the Gentile mission, one can only wonder at the fidelity with which the Church preserved sayings attributed to Jesus that were in such manifest contradiction with the actual course of events. Obviously the saying was not understood in this sense; and it seems most probable that it was understood to refer to the Jewish War of AD 66-70, which elsewhere is associated with the coming of the Son of Man in judgment [→ Chapter 6: (B) Discourse].

24. The persecution of the disciples is explained by a cryptic reference to the passion of Jesus. The saying is preserved in nearly identical form in Jn 13:16; 15:20, referring both to the washing of the feet, which is symbolic of the humility recommended to the disciples, and (as here) to the hatred incurred by the disciples (see also Lk 6:40). Matthew anticipates his own arrangement of the Beelzebul controversy in 12:25-37.

This part of the discourse is, as the parallels show, composed largely of material drawn from Mk, some of which is used twice: in the eschatological discourse (where Mk puts it) and detached from its context here. Matthew selects and so arranges the material because it is a suitable continuation of the missionary discourse.

(ii) Confession without fear (10:26-33)

This collection of sayings comes from Q (cf. Lk 12:2-9); two verses are found in Mk also. 26-27. These verses have a different context from Lk 12:2-3 and quite a different meaning; the saying in Mk 4:22 is closer to the meaning given by Mt. Lk has made the line a warning against the hypocrisy of the Pharisees; it is impossible that "you" should say anything in secret that will not become public; you cannot hide your real mind. Mt refers the saying to the teaching of Jesus. The teaching now reaches only a limited circle, but through the disciples it will be widely published. The saying does not imply that Jesus taught a secret doctrine, but simply that the number who hear his teaching from his own lips is much smaller than the number who will hear it from the disciples.

28. The discourse moves on to a saying in which the prospect of death is stated even more clearly than in the preceding section. The dualism of *sōma* (body) and *psychē* (soul) is unusual in the NT and does not represent the OT conception of the human person. It is remarkable that Luke, presumably a Hellenistic writer, avoids the dualism in his version of the saying; the dualism would be quite germane to several schools of Gk philosophy. *him who can destroy . . . in Gehenna:* God (see comment on 18:8-9). There is a life after one's earthly life that must be preserved. 29. God has as much care for the human person as he has for the sparrow, which was one of the cheapest articles sold in the market. God knows when even a small bird dies; he is aware of the death of one of his own, and he will save the life that endures after death. The variant form of the saying in Lk (21:18) is about the hairs of the head. 32. With this assurance of confidence that God knows and cares what happens, the disciples are urged to confess "in Jesus"; the confession would be the typical confession of the primitive Church that Jesus is Messiah and Lord. The reward of confession or denial is that Jesus will accept or disown according to one's fidelity. A similar saying appears

in Mk 8:38 (Lk 9:26 par.); but the formulation is so dissimilar that it is difficult to assume a common source, unless Matthew has rewritten with great freedom. These sayings are also suitable appendages to the missionary discourse.

(iii) Divided families (10:34–36)

The parallel in Lk (12:51–53) exhibits so many variations that some commentators doubt a common source for the saying; in particular, Lk replaces the vigorous metaphor of the sword with an abstraction. 34. *I have not come to bring peace:* Jesus is of course the messenger of peace in the truest and highest sense of the word; the saying reflects the experience of the primitive Church (see 10:21). The immediate result of the proclamation of the gospel was discord within the Jewish community, which touched even family relations. The same theme is expressed in the words of Simeon (Lk 2:34). The saying is illustrated by the quotation of Mi 7:6 (not according to the LXX, but quite faithful to the MT). The lines lead to the saying in the following verse.

(iv) The renunciation demanded by discipleship (10:37–39)

Cf. Lk 14:26–27 and 17:33; see Mk 8:34–35; Lk 9:23–24. If the gospel introduces a division into families, then the disciple has no choice except to prefer the new community to the community of blood. Mt softens "hate," found in Lk, to "love more"; the language of Lk is closer to the original Aramaic, which had no other way of saying "love less." The example of this renunciation has already been given in the call of the disciples (4:18–22; 9:9–13). 38–39. Two sayings are joined that Lk has in different contexts; but Lk, like Mt, uses the sayings twice (16:24–25). Here again, as in other parts of the discourse, Matthew has used doublets to compile his material. Mk also has the sayings; and the verses are a rare example of sayings found both in Mk and in Q. The very fact that they are quoted so often shows that the early Church, like the modern Church, recognizes these as sayings that express in a remarkably clear manner a basic principle of the gospel and of Christian life. 38. *take up his cross:* This is the first time that Mt uses the word "cross." Other allusions (some have appeared already) to the passion will be found before Jesus predicts it openly. Crucifixion, a method of execution of Oriental origin, was used by the Romans for rebels and for slaves. Roman law prohibited its use on Roman citizens. The conventional use of the cross as a Christian symbol makes it difficult for modern readers to grasp the harshness of this saying as it was originally uttered. Jesus tells the disciples that there is no extreme to which they may think that faith and the proclamation of the gospel will not take them. The personal renunciation implied will go far beyond renunciation of one's own family. 39. The oxymoron assures the disciples that there is no other way in which they can save themselves. The word *psychē*, "soul," is used here in a sense that reflects the OT use (see comment on 10:28). The word should be rendered "self" rather than "soul" or "life." The preservation of the person is achieved only by yielding the person entirely to Jesus. One who saves his life may lose himself.

(v) Conclusion (10:40—11:1)

The final words of the discourse express praise of those who show the disciples hospitality. The praise is based, on the identification of the disciples with Jesus; he is encountered in those who proclaim the gospel. The saying is adapted from Mk 9:37 (see Lk 9:48; Mt 18:5); it is another doublet. 42. *little ones:* The "child" of Mk's saying becomes the plural and refers here to the disciples; they are told to become as little ones in 18:1–4. A similar saying is found in Lk 10:6. The saying about the cup of cold water (Mk 9:41 par.) is aptly placed here because of its association with hospitality.

The concluding verse narrates that Jesus continued his teaching and proclaiming. The mission of the twelve "disciples" is not mentioned again, nor is their return from the mission; the discourse has a somewhat artificial character and situation.

Chapter 4

Book Three

Controversy and Parables (11:2—13:52)

(A) Narrative Section: Incredulity and Hostility of the Jews (11:2—12:50)

(a) The Question of John the Baptist (11:2-6)

THE CORRESPONDENCE BETWEEN MT and Lk (7:18–23) in this and the following sections, except for Mt's omissions, is extremely close; these passages are among the best illustrations of Q. The relations between John the Baptist and his followers and between Jesus and his disciples are somewhat uncertain in the traditions (see 3:13–17). There seems to be little reason for thinking that the question of John was other than sincere, or that he sent his disciples in order to elicit an open profession of messiahship either for their sake or for the sake of a wider public. John was quite capable of expressing his own faith to his own disciples. It is more difficult to explain the reasons why John asked the question. With the little information we have about him, we can surmise that the heavy emphasis on the eschatological judgment the Gospels report in John's preaching (see 3:1–10) did not appear in the proclamation of Jesus, and that this caused John wonder. The messianism and eschatology of John had to be corrected by the proclamation of Jesus. 2. *John in prison*: Mt postpones the explanation of John's imprisonment until the story of his death (14:3–12). According to Josephus (*Ant.*

18.5, 2 § 119), the prison was in the palace-fortress of Machaerus, built by Herod the Great on the desolate heights of Moab near the E central shore of the Dead Sea (JW 7.6, 1–2 § 164–77). *the Coming One:* This title is not attested in Jewish literature for the Messiah, but there could be no doubt of its meaning (see Mal 3:1). 4. Mt has omitted (or Lk has added) a recital of miracles performed in the presence of the disciples of John; this certainly adds vividness to the quotations in which Jesus answers the questions. 5. This verse is not actually a quotation either according to the MT or according to the LXX but a cento of allusions from Is 29:18–19; 35:5–6; 61:1. The raising of the dead is added in Q; it replaces the liberation of captives in Is 61:1. The answer of Jesus, although it is not a formal claim of messiahship, alludes to phenomena that in the OT and Judaism were expected in the Messianic era. More important, the quotations establish the type of messiahship that Jesus lets those see who will look. It is not a messiahship of the eschatological judgment of wrath, nor the establishment of a Messianic empire over all the kingdoms of the earth, nor a war of extermination against the enemies of the elect people. The messiahship here suggested is a messiahship of the healing of ills and the conferring of blessing. 6. *not be scandalized:* The *skandalon* is anything over which one stumbles and falls; the use both of the noun and the verb in the NT is exclusively metaphorical to designate something that makes faith difficult; see 18:6–9. That this type of messiahship was a scandal even to the disciples of Jesus is abundantly clear from the Gospels.

(b) The Witness of Jesus to John the Baptist (11:7–19)

Except for the insertion of 11:12 (Lk 16:16 par.) from a different context, Mt and Lk still are very close. The witness of Jesus to John is given both to John's manner of life and to his genuine prophetic mission. 9. *to see a prophet:* In Jewish belief prophecy had ended with the closing of the canon of the prophetic books, and the next prophet to appear would be the prophet "like Moses" (Dt 18:15). 10. This is clearly the meaning of the witness that Jesus gives to John; Jesus applies to John the text of Mal 3:1 (quoted according to the MT), one of the texts on which the belief in the "Coming One" was based. This makes John the last and the greatest of the prophets; but Jesus calls him even more: the greatest figure of the dispensation of the Law and the prophets. By implication John is greater even than Moses. *is greater than he:* John lived and worked before the reign. Therefore even the least in the reign, who will have the light of the gospel and the communication of the power of faith, will accomplish greater works than John.

12. This verse is obscure in both Mt and Lk (16:16); and it is hard to say whether Lk has compressed a difficult sentence or Mt has expanded it to explain it. It may mean either "the reign does violence" or "the reign suffers violence." In the first meaning the reign is said to make a violent entrance into the world (see 10:34), and those seize it as a prize who are willing to be as violent as the reign demands—by the kind of renunciation Jesus imposes upon his disciples. Many interpreters find this sense somewhat forced; they prefer to say simply that the reign has always been under the violent attack of its enemies and is now under attack. This interpretation does not fit well with the word "snatch" or "carry off"—a word that is used in Greek of taking plunder. Another possibility relates the verse to the contemporary scene and identifies the violent with the party of the Zealots (see comment on 10:4), who sought to establish the reign by violence. No proposed interpretation is entirely satisfactory. Mt's interpretation of the discourse, because of the occurrence of the name of John in 11:12, is somewhat violent itself. 13. *prophesied until John*: Mt returns to the topic, reaffirming that John terminates the Law and the prophets. 14. *he is Elijah*: Cf. Mal 3:1,22; *Elias redivivus*. The messianic prophet was sometimes identified with Elijah returning; Elijah had never died but was carried off in a chariot (2 Kgs 2:11–12). This statement is repeated in 17:10–13 in a longer form. 15. *let him who has ears hear*: A tag used when a cryptic saying is proposed; it was a sign of the wise man that he could speak in riddles and solve them.

16–19. The first indication in Mt of a wide disbelief in the proclamation of Jesus; it is the sole indication of remarks directed against John the Baptist, respect for whom is attested both in the Gospels and in Josephus (*Ant.* 18.5, 2 § 116–19). Jesus and John followed quite diverse manners of life. John was a hermit who reduced his use of material goods to an absolute minimum. Jesus, although he was poor and preached renunciation, made no similar radical departure from the usual manner of life of the Jews. The austere prophet was called a demoniac; the rabbi who lived much like other rabbis was called a glutton and a drunkard who liked low company. No approach could satisfy the Jews if it suggested a change in their belief and their life. Jesus uses the homely parable of children who always want to play some other game than the one suggested by their companions. 19b. *wisdom is justified by her deeds*: Another obscure saying. It is probably proverbial and would make good sense in the wisdom tradition, in which wisdom is proved genuine both by the success of the wise man (Prv 3:13-18) and by the wisdom he teaches his children (Prv 10:1). But precisely what Jesus means by wisdom here is not clear. Most obviously it is the divine wisdom, which in one reading proves itself by its works and in the other reading by those who accept it— here, the disciples of Jesus. Some interpreters think that the Church has formed the saying and that Jesus himself is meant by wisdom; he too is proved both by his deeds and by his disciples. Lk 7:35 reads "by her children," a reading that has also contaminated the Matthaean ms. tradition.

(c) Doom of the Cities of Galilee (11:20-24)

This passage is from Q. Luke makes it a part of the farewell words of Jesus to Galilee; Matthew probably saw an opportunity to contrast the praise of John the Baptist with the reproach delivered against those who had seen much more of Jesus than John had. 21. *Chorazin, Bethsaida, Capernaum*: Of the three towns mentioned Mt has related no miracles except for Capernaum. Chorazin appears only here and in Lk 11:13. It is identified with Khirbet Kerazeh, about 2 mi. NW of Tell Hum, the site of Capernaum. Bethsaida is the home of Peter, Andrew, and Philip in Jn 1:44, the scene of the healing of a blind man in Mk 8:22, and near the place of the multiplication of the loaves in Mk 6:45; Lk 9:10. The name seems to have belonged to a fishing village on the shore of the Sea of Galilee and to a new city, 2 mi. N of the sea and E of the Jordan, founded by the tetrarch Philip. For Capernaum, see comment on 4:13. *would have repented*: The people of these towns have not done so. In spite of the works of power they had seen, repentance was a part of the proclamation of Jesus (4:17). Plainly the works of power should have moved them to faith. 22. *Tyre and Sidon*: These towns were not eminent examples of wickedness; they were Gentile cities that were near. 23. *Capernaum*: The object of a peculiar reproach, for it was the city of Jesus (9:1); Mt has expanded the reproach by repeating vv. 21-22 and by comparing Capernaum not to Tyre and Sidon but to the outstanding proverbial example of wickedness in the OT, Sodom. *exalted to heaven*: The words of Is 14:13,15 are adapted to Capernaum. On the basis of this and similar passages elsewhere it must be concluded that the mission of Jesus in Galilee produced only a few disciples. The mass of the population was interested—all the Gospels refer to crowds attracted by Jesus—but they remained unmoved by the proclamation.

BOOK THREE: CONTROVERSY AND PARABLES (11:2—13:52)

(d) Thanksgiving to the Father (11:25-27)

This passage also is from Q. The verbal correspondence of Mt and Lk is nearly perfect except for Mt's omission of a phrase in v. 25 and a merely grammatical variation in v. 27. Lk places the saying after the return of the 72 disciples; it is a prayer of thanksgiving for the success of their mission and for the understanding that has been granted to them, "the little ones." The position of the saying in Mt—after the reproach of the Galilean cities—contrasts the little ones, the disciples, with the wise and prudent, who are the Jews, in particular their spiritual leaders, the scribes and Pharisees. 26. *such was your good pleasure*: The tone of thanksgiving mixed with resignation is, however, apparent in the form of the saying itself; for resignation is expressed in v. 26. Jesus has not reached the wise and prudent; his message has been grasped only by a few disciples who are drawn from the peasant and working classes. But this is the work of the Father. The message of Jesus is not grasped by wisdom and understanding; it is known only by revelation. The saying does not mean that revelation has been denied to the wise and prudent in the Jewish community; Jesus has proclaimed the reign, and this is revelation. But only the simple have accepted the insight the Father grants to those who wish it. There is a sense in which Jewish wisdom and learning, which was the knowledge of the Law, was a genuine obstacle to the understanding of the message of Jesus. The more one knew about the Law, the more difficult it was to see that the messianic revolution would supersede the Law; see 5:17-20.

27. *all things have been given over to me by my father*: This verse is so singular in the Syn that it has been the object of many conjectures; it has been called "a meteor from the Johannine heaven." The intimate relation of Jesus and the Father is mentioned frequently in Jn, rarely in the Syn. But the saying is as well attested in Q as anything in the Gospels; we have noticed that the correspondence of Mt and Lk is unusually close. The saying is formal, even labored, particularly in Mt. Jesus claims that "all" has been handed over by the Father; in the context "all" probably means revelation. *knows the son*: The prerogative of the Father; only by the revelation of the Father can the true identity of the Son be recognized (11:25; and see 16:17). Conversely, only the Son can reveal the Father. In the context this is a direct contradiction of the Jewish claim to have the complete revelation of God in the Law and the Prophets. The saying fills out the implications in the usual way in which Jesus speaks of the Father; he has a relation with the

Father that other men do not share. (See A. Feuillet, *RB* 62 [1955] 161–96; A. Gelin [ed.], *Son and Saviour* [Baltimore, 1962] 77–78.)

(e) Invitation to the Weary (11:28–30)

This saying is peculiar to Mt. But since the studies of E. Norden in 1913, some commentators have been convinced that the triple strophe which can be seen in 25–30, and which is paralleled elsewhere, is the original form. One can hardly imagine why Lk would have omitted these verses, which are so much in harmony with the themes of his Gospel. If Mt has the original form, the saying must have come to Lk already mutilated. 28. *the weary and the burdened:* Those who are under the "yoke" of the Law; the metaphor of the yoke is used in rabbinical writings. In this context perhaps this suggestion is intended. But the import of the saying in itself is more general; the weary and the burdened are the poor (see 5:3–5), who have the good news proclaimed to them (11:5). Jesus invites them because he is one of them; the adjectives used in 11:29 are identical in meaning and very close verbally to the adjectives of the first and third beatitudes (5:3,5). 29. *take my yoke:* The yoke and the burden of Jesus are submission to the reign of God. This imposes no further burden on those who accept it, but rather makes it easier for them to bear the burdens they already have. Jer 6:16 (quoted according to the MT) promises rest to those who follow "the old paths," the traditions of Israel. This saying flows easily from the preceding claim of a unique relation of sonship. The revelation of the Father is not conceived as the revelation of new obligations but as a knowledge of the Father that releases from burdens and weariness and makes it easier to live under his will.

(f) Sabbath Controversy: Plucking Corn (12:1–8)

Most of the remaining episodes in this book resume the theme of controversy begun in 9:1–8. The order followed is the order of Mk except for the insertion of some material from Q. The first two controversies deal with the Sabbath. The incident of the plucking of ears on the Sabbath illustrates the "saying-story." It appears that the original material consisted only of the sayings in Mk 2:27–28. Of these sayings Mt retains only one. The dialogue is constructed in the framework of a dispute that is resolved by the sayings. 1. *through the fields:* The journey is presented as a trip to the synagogue on the Sabbath (12:9). The disciples plucked ears of wheat and rubbed the

BOOK THREE: CONTROVERSY AND PARABLES (11:2—13:52)

grains in their hands to make a rough meal; Lk found it necessary to make this explicit for his readers. The preparation of food was listed by the rabbis as one of the 39 forms of work that were forbidden on the Sabbath; the inclusion of such an action as that of the disciples illustrates the rigorist school of Pharisaic interpretation. The plucking of stray ears in a field, permitted in Dt 23:26, was prohibited by the rabbis on the Sabbath.

3. The answer of Jesus is twofold; and like a good rabbinical argument it is based on the Scripture. The first example is the story of David (1 Sm 21:2–7); he and his men ate the showbread (Lv 24:5–9) in the Tabernacle because they had no other food. The second example is given only in Mt, which elsewhere in this passage follows Mk more closely than usual. 5. *how the priests . . . profane the Sabbath:* The work of the priests in the Temple is "work" in the rabbinical sense, but it is justified by its holy purpose. The application to the disciples is obvious, but much more suggestive than the version of Mk. The disciples of Jesus may work on the Sabbath in his company because this service is greater than the service of the Temple. Mt turns the dispute into a Messianic affirmation. 7. This verse, also peculiar to Mt, quotes again Hos 6:6 (quoted in 9:13) in support of the humanitarian interpretation of the Law. Rigorism is condemnation of the innocent. Thus the two answers are a plea for a humanitarian interpretation of the Law and a claim that Jesus is greater than the Law. The example of David does support this interpretation, but is does not apply directly to the Sabbath. 8. The saying is ambiguous, even though the omission of Mk 2:27 makes it less so. Mk 2:27 is a bold statement of the humanitarian view; the Sabbath law is to be interpreted according to human needs and possibilities. *Son of Man:* If this phrase is to be interpreted as "man" (a sense that the Aram equivalent will bear), the saying is synonymous with Mk 2:27. This, however, is probably not the meaning of the sentence. It is not a claim that the Sabbath is under the decision of man, but that it is under the decision of Jesus. The episode in all three Gospels lies in the same pattern of thought we see in Mt 5:17–48. Jesus is the supreme interpreter of the Law; and he interprets it in humanitarian terms. The Sabbath law does not oblige one to go hungry.

(g) Sabbath Controversy: Healing (12:9–14)

Lk (6:6–11) has not only a parallel to this passage, but two other incidents of healing on the Sabbath (13:10–17; 14:1–6), which illustrate the same principle. The controversy about the Sabbath was sufficiently important to appear in both Mk and Q and perhaps in independent sources. Mt makes the Pharisees inquire of Jesus instead of observe him; and the challenge uttered by Jesus to their unspoken question becomes a challenge uttered by the Pharisees. 11. This verse (Lk 14:5 par.), missing in Mk, may have had no context in a miracle story in Q. Rabbinical practice as attested in the Talmud did permit one to render assistance to an animal on the Sabbath; but the Talmud also attests a more rigorous view that apparently did not prevail in NT times (Str-B 1, 629–30); but cf. CD 11:13–14. 12. The argument proceeds from the superiority of man to animals. Rabbinical opinion generally permitted the practice of healing on the Sabbath if there was danger of death, but not if the healing could be postponed until the next day (Str-B 1, 622–29). This practice is so much in agreement with modern medical and hospital practice on Sundays and holidays that it scarcely calls for comment. 13. Jesus, however, affirms by the miracle that it is permitted to do good on the Sabbath whether the work can be postponed or not. Matthew abbreviates Mk by omitting any reference to the anger and grief of Jesus (Mk 3:5). 14. He also omits the mention of the Herodians (Mk 3:6) as partners with the Pharisees. If the omission here is due to the fact that the party had long ceased to exist when the Gospel was written, this motive was not operative in the composition of 22:16. The omission is more probably another abbreviation. The movement is climactic; this is the first mention of a plot against the life of Jesus.

The theme of the story is the same humanitarian interpretation of the Sabbath as that of the preceding incident. The first example illustrates self-help on the Sabbath, the second example illustrates assistance rendered to others.

(h) Jesus the Servant of the Lord (12:15–21)

Matthew has sharply reduced the material in this passage where Mk (3:7–12) summarizes the mission of Jesus in Galilee. Matthew has given a similar summary in 4:23–25. The purpose of the summary here is to introduce the quotation from Is 42:1–4, which is introduced by another of Matthew's rare allusions to Mk's "Messianic Secret" (see 8:4). Matthew here takes account of the secret, but he explains it as a "fulfillment" (see comment on 1:18–25) of Is 42:1–4. The passage is quoted not according to the LXX but according to the MT translated very freely. The identification of Jesus with the Servant of the Lord of Dt-Is was a key idea in the Gospels and of

Book Three: Controversy and Parables (11:2—13:52)

the primitive Church. Matthew has already quoted one Servant passage, which is applied to Jesus in a very broad sense (see 8:17). Here the passage is quoted not with reference to the mission of Jesus to proclaim the reign, but as an explanation of his retirement from proclaiming before a wider public. 15. *knowing*: The motive for the retirement is given by Mt alone in this one obscure word; the implicit object of the participle is the plot mentioned in v. 14. The quotation from Dt-Is refers clearly to a mission of the Servant to the Gentiles, and Matthew includes this in his quotation. These passages are relevant in the interpretation of such passages as 10:5; 15:24. The quotation in which the Servant passage is applied to Jesus is very probably intended as a striking contrast to the accusation of the Pharisees reported in the following passage.

(i) The Accusation of the Pharisees (12:22–24)

The accusation of the Pharisees is the occasion of one of the major controversial statements of Jesus (see the following passage). The accusation is found in Mk (3:20–22) without the miracle story; both Mt and Lk (11:14–16) have the miracle story from Q; and it seems that the accusation also followed the miracle story in Q. The miracle is described in only the bare essentials; the interest is not in the miracle but in the discussion that follows. 22. *a blind and dumb demoniac*: Mt adds "blind" to the "dumb" of Lk. The description illustrates the current popular demonology (see comment on 8:28–34). Where Lk has a question expressing wonder, Mt has a question whether Jesus is not the Son of David, a Messianic title. Mt specifies the accusers as Pharisees; Mk has "the scribes," Lk "some." We have noticed that Mt anticipates this incident in 9:32–34. 24. *Beelzebul*: The name comes from 2 Kgs 1:2-6. The NT has preserved the correct reading of the name; the MT has corrupted it (a not infrequent occurrence when divine names occur in the MT) to *Ba'alzᵉbûb*. The name means "Baal the prince" and is not attested elsewhere in Jewish literature as the name of a demon (cf. W. Foerster, *ThDNT* 1, 605–6). The accusation reduces Jesus to the level of a common magician; it was understood that such feats could be performed with the assistance of demons.

(j) Response to the Accusation (12:25–37)

A comparison of the three Syn shows that this episode was found both in Mk (3:23–30) and in Q (Lk 11:17–23; 12:10 par.). This indicates the importance this discussion had in the early Church; and it is altogether probable that the composition of the passage reflects the controversies of the primitive Church with the Jews. Verses 25–26 are an abbreviation of Mk 3:23–26, but vv. 27–28 agree with Lk 11:18a–20 with no parallel in Mk. Verse 30 agrees with Lk 11:23, again with no parallel in Mk. Verses 31–32 conflate Mk 3:28–29 and a Q passage that appears in a briefer form in Lk 12:10. Verses 33–36 are an expansion peculiar to Mt [→ Chapter 4: (A) Narrative section: (j) Response to the Accusation: 33–37].

25. *a kingdom divided against itself:* The first argument in response is based on the absurdity of the charge of the Pharisees. If Jesus expels demons by Beelzebul, then the kingdom of Satan is doomed by its own internecine strife. This consequence the Pharisees are unwilling to admit. Implicit, no doubt, is the principle that the collapse of the reign of Satan will not occur until the advent of the reign of God. 27. The second argument, missing in Mk, is drawn from exorcisms worked by Jews. *your sons:* A Semitism for "yourselves," "members of your own group." The genuineness of the exorcisms worked by Jews is not called in question; it is neither affirmed nor denied. There is a subtlety in this argument that eludes the modern reader; our ignorance of the ritual of Jewish exorcisms makes the force of the argument somewhat difficult to see. The exorcisms of Jesus in the Gospels are accomplished by a simple command, sometimes accompanied by a touch. It is highly probable that Jewish exorcists used long and complicated rituals, with perhaps more than a touch of magical formulas. 27. *they will be your judges:* Jesus challenges the Pharisees to compare the displays of power. Jewish exorcists themselves will be the judges; they can attest the implications of a successful exorcism performed by a simple command. 28. *God's Spirit:* The power of Jesus shows that the spirit of God is at work; Lk 11:20 has the more picturesque "finger" of God (see Ex 8:15). Lk's phrase is probably more original; Mt's change to "spirit" leads into the saying about blasphemy, which Lk has in a different context (12:10). *the reign of God has overtaken you:* Lit., "has come upon you," i.e., when they were not looking. Such a display of the power of the Spirit clearly shows that the Messianic age is dawning. This Messianic claim is more explicit than Mk's customary style.

Book Three: Controversy and Parables (11:2—13:52)

29. The parable of the strong man shows that Jesus is completely master of the demons. Satan is a robber lord whose "goods," which means here those who are bound by demonic possession, are kept in his castle. No one can release them unless he has mastered the strong one and his fortress. 30. Here Q added a saying that is not found in Mk and does not seem to belong to this context. A similar idea is expressed in Mk 9:40; Lk 9:50. The saying affirms that Jesus demands a decision that cannot be evaded. Neutrality toward him is impossible; to be neutral is to reject him.

31. *blasphemy against the Spirit*: The saying about blasphemy against the Spirit has long presented difficulty, particularly in Catholic theology, which affirms the possibility of repentance up to the moment of death. This teaching is solidly founded in the NT, and this saying of Jesus cannot be understood in a way that contradicts his invitations to repentance. Refusal to recognize the Son of Man as Messiah can be forgiven; faith atones for previous denial of faith. This Messianic claim is missing in Mk. Blasphemy against the Holy Spirit, however, attributes the activity of the Spirit to some other power. The present activity of God can be attested only through the actions of the Spirit. If these are not recognized, then there is no means by which God can reach man. The one who will not accept the work of the Spirit has made it impossible for himself to recognize the word and the work of God. Only he can be forgiven who confesses that he has something to be forgiven.

33-37. These verses are an expansion of Matthew composed from a passage of Q that is at the base both of Lk 6:43-45 and Mt 7:16-20; the passage adapted to the present context to describe the dogmatic unbelief of the Pharisees. 34. *brood of vipers*: See 3:7; 23:33. The sayings all touch upon the theme of speech as revealing the genuine character of the person. Speech is the fruit that discloses whether the tree is good or bad. The evil person cannot speak good things; for speech is the overflow of the heart. *out of the abundance of the heart*: The heart in the Bible generally is not the organ of sentiment, as it is in our metaphorical language, but rather the mind and the sentiments. Even the hypocrite cannot long conceal his real convictions. Goodness or wickedness will manifest itself in word. 36. The final saying is peculiar to Mt; its severity is apparent, but the entire context is couched in a severe tone. *idle word*: This does not mean merely the trivial or unnecessary word; it is the word spoken without foundation, the word that serves no purpose. Such a word may be mendacious or calumnious simply because the speaker has not reflected on the content and implications of his speech. The saying echoes the ancient conception of word as an existent and dynamic reality. If the reality the speaker creates is an agent of evil, the speaker must accept full responsibility for the evil. It was in his power to speak with reflection.

(k) Signs (12:38–42)

The present passage is based on Q (Lk 11:29–32 par.) with a distinctive adaptation of Mt. A similar request for a sign is found in Mk 8:11–12 (cf. 16:1–4; Matthew has again used the same or similar material in two different passages). 38. *a sign:* The "sign" in the OT was an extraordinary or paradoxical event that manifested the present activity of God (see Is 7:10). Isaiah invites Ahaz to ask a sign as deep as Sheol or as high as heaven; some phenomenon in nature is clearly indicated. When the king refuses the challenge, Isaiah gives him the sign of the birth of a child. The essential feature of the sign is not its marvelous character but its significance; it is an event that admits an obvious interpretation. In the context the request is directed toward a Messianic sign, the type of event that in Jewish belief would precede the coming of the Messiah; see 24:3. The Beelzebul controversy is thus followed by an indirect, but not subtle, demand for a verification of the Messianic claims. 39. *a wicked and adulterous generation:* "Adulterous," which echoes an OT metaphor for the infidelity of Israel (see Jer 2:1–3,20–25,32–33; 3:1–5; Hos 2:3–22), does not appear in Lk. In Lk there are two parallel signs, the repentance of the Ninevites at the proclamation of Jonah (Jon 3:5) and the journey of the queen of Sheba (in southern Arabia, "the ends of the earth" in ancient geography) to hear the wisdom of Solomon. In these instances the Gentiles exhibited repentance and an eagerness to hear the wisdom that Yahweh gave; the Pharisees show neither of these attitudes. The theme of the faith of the Gentiles in contrast to the unbelief of Israel is repeated. 40. This addition in Mt alters the significance of the sign of Jonah. The repentance of the Ninevites is a sign that the unbelieving Jews will be judged; the sojourn of Jonah in the belly of the whale for three days and three nights (Jon 2:1) is a foreshadowing of the resurrection of Jesus. This will be the sign the Pharisees seek. Matthew anticipates his own account of the resurrection, which emphasizes the refusal of the Jews to accept this sign. No sign can be given them, for they have blasphemed against the Holy Spirit. (See A. Vögtle, "Der Spruch vom Jonaszeichen," *Synoptische Studien* [Fest. A. Wikenhauser; Munich, 1953] 230–77.)

BOOK THREE: CONTROVERSY AND PARABLES (11:2—13:52)

(l) The Return of the Evil Spirit (12:43-45)

This saying from Q is preserved in a very close verbal parallel in Mt and Lk (11:24-26). The force of the saying is obscure. In Lk it is arranged in closer connection with the Beelzebul controversy. The saying casts some light on exorcisms performed in NT times (see 12:27); the cure was sometimes only temporary, and the patient relapsed into a worse condition. This should certainly cause no surprise when we recall that many pathological conditions were attributed to demons, and any apparent cure could be only the work of suggestion. The saying may have originally been intended to contrast the healings and exorcisms of Jesus with the merely temporary results achieved by other exorcists. 43. *waterless places:* The expelled demon wanders through the desert, in the Bible the home of evil spirits (see 4:1; Is 32:21; 34:14; Tb 8:3). There he finds seven like himself; when all return to the man whom he previously haunted, they find the dwelling swept and clean—but empty. The demonic power has not been replaced by power for good. 45. *with this evil generation:* In Mt the figure is explicitly applied to the Jews. The Jews have experienced the coming of the reign that expels the reign of Satan. The power of Satan has been rolled back, but the Jews have not accepted the reign of God. Nothing can happen but another and stronger invasion of the power of Satan.

(m) The Brethren of Jesus (12:46-50)

In Mk (3:31-35) this passage is probably a resumption of Mk 3:20-21, a passage so difficult that both Mt and Lk omit it. "His own" (so we may render Mk 3:21) are here specified as his mother and brethren. 46. *brothers:* This word must be taken as kinsmen, unless one insists that Mary had children who are never mentioned in the NT or in any other source of early tradition (see comments on 1:25). The kinsmen, very probably from Nazareth, seem to have felt that Jesus was acting imprudently. Most commentators have failed to regard the kinsmen as being kind; the allusions in the Gospels to the hostility of the Pharisees are to be taken seriously, and it is more likely that the kinsmen were motivated by a desire to take Jesus out of a situation of growing danger than by envy or fear for his sanity. 47. This verse is not attested in the most important mss. and is largely a repetition of 12:46. 48. Matthew has here abbreviated so sharply that he becomes obscure. The response of Jesus seems harsh, but it is not harsher than his words in 8:22 and 10:37, which are here illustrated by his conduct. The new unity Jesus forms about himself is a unity in which other bonds, even the bonds of kinship, are sublimated. Jesus does not reject the bonds of kinship, but raises all who believe in him to an intimacy of kinship. His own kin exclude themselves from this new unity if they do not believe in him. Again in fairness to the kinsmen, the saying does not imply that they do not believe in Jesus.

(B) Discourse: The Parables of the Reign (13:1–52)

The parable in the NT designates a wise saying or fictitious short story used by Jesus to expound his teaching. The roots of these literary forms lie in the OT, particularly in the wisdom literature, and in the rabbinical literature (Str-B 1, 653–55). The fictitious anecdote leads the listener to concede a point that he does not immediately perceive is applicable to himself (see 2 Sm 12:1–14; 14:1–11; 1 Kgs 20:35–40). The story also sharpens the curiosity and attracts attention. The rabbinical parables, of which about 2000 are counted in rabbinical literature, are told in answer to the question of a disciple and show that the scope of the answer is broader than the disciple perceived. These purposes are all apparent in the parables of Jesus.

For most of the parables of the Gospels it is possible to find a situation in the life and teaching of Jesus himself and a situation in the life and teaching of the primitive community. The parables were modified in the teaching of the community; such modifications can be seen by comparing different versions of the same parable in different Gospels. The commentaries on the parables (see 13:18–23,36–43) and most allegorical features are almost universally regarded by modern scholars as expansions made by the primitive Church. Other modifications include the creation of a new setting for the parable and the addition of a saying of Jesus.

(a) The Parable of the Sower (13:1–9)

The collection of parables is one of the two extended discourses in Mk, and Mt uses the entire collection except for Mk 4:26–29, adding other parables drawn both from Q and from a private source. Matthew abbreviates Mk less in the discourses than in the narratives; here he follows Mk in placing the teaching in a boat by the seashore; Lk alters the scene.

3. This parable is a simple description of the process of plowing in Palestine, of the type of ground upon which seed is sown, and of the usual results. The "road" is not the highway, but the soil trodden hard in paths through the fields. The wild thorns, the most common weed in the country, are not cleared before plowing but turned under by the plow. The fields are sown throughout, even in the edges and corners where the limestone base lies very near the surface. Verse 9 is a saying that indicates that the preceding utterance has more than a superficial meaning (see comment on 11:15).

Setting aside for the moment the explanation given in the Gospel (13:18–23), one observes that 13:8 is a very apt conclusion. Modern interpreters are at variance on the meaning of the parable, possibly because they try to give the parable a more precise meaning than it was intended to convey. The reign (or the proclamation of the reign) is certainly the central theme of the parable. The reign will arrive in spite of obstacles; it is as infallible as the growth of the harvest, which reaches maturity and even richness in spite of what seem to be nearly insuperable difficulties. One perceives the optimism that should inspire the preachers of the Gospel and is assured that such opponents as the Pharisees in the present context will not prevail; these responses are inferred, not stated. The parable is presented as a theme on which one can reflect and from which one can draw as much meaning as one wishes: on this basis the earliest explanation of the parable (18–23) was composed.

(b) The Parables as Revelation (13:10–15)

Mt omits Mk's notice (4:10) that this explanation was given when Jesus was alone with the disciples; but the character of the explanation remains the same. The reason for parables as given in Mk seems extremely harsh, and in both Mt and Lk it is softened—in Mt by altering the syntax and expanding the passage, in Lk by reducing the passage so sharply that it becomes nearly incomprehensible. 11. An implicit difference between the general patterns of Mk and Mt is pertinent here: in Mk the disciples are represented as not understanding the preaching of Jesus until the final moment, whereas in Mt this theme of obtuseness is much less perceptible. That knowledge is "given" to the disciples and withheld from "them" (Mk has "those outside," but the omission seems not to alter the meaning) is not due to a refusal to give, but to a refusal to receive. 12. *to him who has more will be given*: Mt expands the saying by transferring Mk 4:25 to this point: he who has (= receives) the reign shall receive more; he who has not (= refuses) the reign shall lose what he has (for the Jews, their position as the chosen people who have received the revelation of God). 13. *because seeing they do not see:* The harshness of Mk 4:12 is due to the use of a Gk particle expressing purpose (*hina*); this reflects an ambiguity implicit in Hebrew and Aramaic, which do not distinguish grammatically between purpose and result (*GrBib* § 351–53). Indeed, biblical writers could scarcely conceive of a divine purpose that did not achieve its result nor of the result of a divine action that was not from a purpose. 14. The formulation of Mk 4:12 is based on Is 6:9–10; Mt again eases the harshness by quoting the text in full in a "fulfillment" formula; see 1:22. This is the longest explicit quotation in Mt, and it follows the LXX exactly except for one word; some interpreters believe that it is an extremely early expansion of the Gospel. Obscurity cannot be entirely removed here; the basic problem is the problem of obduracy, which ultimately has no perfectly rational explanation. In the biblical conception denial of faith becomes itself the punishment of denial of faith. In Mt the saying fits his general pattern of the growing hostility of the Pharisees to Jesus; in a sense they have already reached the peak of unbelief in the Beelzebul controversy (12:25–37) and have closed their eyes and ears to any communication. The ultimate problem in the passage is not the meaning and the purpose of the parables, but the problem of the refusal of the Jews to accept their Messiah. For this reason most commentators think the saying has its original context in none of the Gospels.

(c) The Blessing of Faith (13:16–17)

Luke (10:23–24) places this saying from Q immediately after the thanksgiving of Jesus for the Father's revelation to the simple (see 11:25–27); he thus connects it with the revelation. Matthew's use is not an alteration. He uses the catchwords "see" and "hear" from 13:13 to identify the disciples as those who, unlike the unbelieving Jews, perceive the revelation of the reign. 17. *prophets and righteous:* These terms occur together in 10:41 and in 23:29; strangely both in 23:29 and here Lk does not have the same pair. Lk is probably closer to the source, for it is difficult to see why "righteous" should be altered to "kings."

Book Three: Controversy and Parables (11:2—13:52)

(d) The Interpretation of the Parable of the Sower (13:18-23)

This passage is now generally regarded by commentators as the interpretation given the parable by the primitive Christian community. We may thus call it a second level of interpretation; the first level is of a more general character. The second level proceeds by allegorizing. The terms of the allegory reflect the conditions of the primitive Church rather than the proclamation of the reign by Jesus, and this so clearly that there is little room for doubt that the Church is interpreting the parable. This interpretation does not annihilate the first level of interpretation but rather builds upon it. The soil represents various types of members of the Church, those who have heard the Gospel and accepted it with faith. But the faith is not always persevering.

18. Mt softens Mk 4:13, which includes the disciples among those who do not understand the parables. 19. *the word of the reign*: This is the seed. *do not understand*: A phrase peculiar to Mt; this does not signify intellectual apprehension, but the full acceptance of the Gospel. *the wicked one* (see comment on 6:13). He easily "snatches" the word. 20. *hears and receives with joy*: This is synonymous with "understand" in v. 19. This second class are "opportunists" who cannot meet the challenge of suffering and persecution. 22. *the cares of the world*: The third class also hears and accepts, but is distracted by secular interests. 23. The fourth class hears, understands, and performs. Each of the classes illustrates the sayings of Jesus in the Gospels about the word of the Gospel; the interpretation is not original but is a synthesis of Gospel material. It is not without interest that the primitive community was able so early to classify its delinquent members. Mt's revision of Mk is quite extensive in this passage, but the revisions are intended for clarity rather than for any alteration of the sense. The abbreviations are few, in contrast to Lk, which abbreviates the passage much more sharply.

(e) The Parable of the Darnel (13:24-30)

Matthew omits the parable of the seed that grows secretly (Mk 4:26-29) and gives this parable instead, peculiar to himself. 25. *darnel*: The weed, "tares" or "cockle" in the older Eng versions, is commonly recognized as darnel, a weed that has a resemblance to wheat. This parable is explained in vv. 36-43. The form of the parable does not allow a statement of the first level of interpretation [→ Chapter 4: (B) Discourse: (d) The Interpretation of the Parable of the Sower]. The composition of the parable in its present form reflects the experience of the primitive community.

(f) The Parable of the Mustard Seed (13:31–32)

The mustard seed must have been proverbially small (see 17:20); but it is not the smallest of seeds, nor is the tree (more properly a shrub, which grows to a height of 10–12 ft.) remarkably tall. The point of the parable is the contrast. **32.** *nest in its branches:* These words are based on Dn 4:21, but on no existing Gk version. No allegorical explanation is given, but it would be quite easy to form one. Without allegory the parable signifies the arrival of the reign from beginnings so small that they are hardly perceptible. The humble beginning of the reign in Jesus was a scandal to Judaism and even to his own disciples.

(g) The Parable of the Leaven (13:33)

This parable is found in Q (Lk 18:20–21 par.). In its present form it falls into the same pattern with the parables of the sower and the mustard seed, illustrating again the irresistible growth of the reign from small beginnings. *three measures of meal:* The size of the lump of dough is exaggerated to make the point. Leaven, mentioned rarely in the NT, is used only in this passage as a figure of something good (see 16:6; 1 Cor 5:6–8; Gal 5:9). It is possible that the original saying has a force something like that of 1 Cor 5:6, and that it was given a different meaning when it was incorporated into the collection of the parables of the reign.

(h) Speaking in Parables (13:34–35)

In Mk these lines are the conclusion to the collection of parables; Matthew follows the order of Mk (4:33–34), even though he adds other parables. He omits Mk's allusions to the inability of the crowds to understand and to the explanation given privately to the disciples. This agrees with his treatment of Mk 4:10–12 (see 13:10–15). The parables are a form of revelation, not of concealment. The point is further expanded by a fulfillment quotation (see comment on 1:22). The text quoted is called the words of a prophet, although the source is Ps 78:2; David is called a prophet in Acts 2:30. The

BOOK THREE: CONTROVERSY AND PARABLES (11:2—13:52)

text follows neither the MT nor the LXX; it is freely adapted to fit the revelation of Jesus.

(i) The Interpretation of the Parable of the Darnel (13:36–43)

The explanation is entirely allegorical; but even with the explanation the parable and the allegory raise questions. It has been noticed above that the form of the parable is such that it suits the allegorical explanation; and thus it seems likely that the parable is either composed by Matthew or his sources or it is a substantial reworking of a parable of Jesus. 38. *the field is the world*: The scandals and the workers of lawlessness are collected from "the kingdom of the Son of Man." This must mean the Church. The problem is not the existence of the wicked in the world at large, but the existence of wicked men where the Son of Man has sown good men; the seed is the members of the Church, not the word. 39. The solution to the problem is purely eschatological. The angels are the ministers of judgment (see 13:49; 24:31). The Church has come to recognize that it is not entirely a community of the elect; it has unfaithful members. God will tolerate such members in the Church as he tolerates them in the world at large; but the judgment will determine the final destiny of righteous and wicked and will purify the kingdom entirely. The lesson is certainly one of patient tolerance of the presence of the wicked even in the community of the reign. 43. To the explanation is added the phrase, "Let him who has ears hear," which is elsewhere attached to the parable itself. The explanation is not entirely consistent with itself; possibly it shows more than one level of interpretation.

(j) The Parables of the Treasure and the Pearl (13:44–46)

These parables, peculiar to Mt, have a common theme. Where the other parables speak of the reign and of its members as a group, these parables are addressed to the individual person. In both, the man sells all he has (see 19:21). The reign demands total renunciation (6:24; 8:18–22; 10:37–39). Here the emphasis is less on the renunciation than on the supreme value of the reign; renunciation has its reward. Small hoards of coins and jewelry are still found occasionally in Palestine both by chance and by archaeological exploration. In the unsettled ancient world when the danger of foreign invasion or brigandage was almost always present, many a householder buried his little store in the hope of a return, which he never made. The finder of the treasure does not tell the owner of the field; Jesus passes no judgment on the ethics of the finder, but uses his avarice as an example of the zeal with which the believer should pursue the reign at any price. The pearl merchant similarly puts all his possessions in one investment that he knows will repay him handsomely.

(k) The Parable of the Net (13:47–50)

This parable, also peculiar to Mt, is very close to the parable of the darnel (24–30,36–43). The theme of the presence of both good and wicked in the Church is even clearer here, and the eschatological solution is identical. In this parable, however, it is possible to trace an earlier form of the parable beneath the allegorizing second level of interpretation. The introductory verse makes no mention of good or wicked, but states simply "from every kind." The reign is thus described as universal in its scope and excluding no one. The net (Gk *sagēnē*) is the large dragnet. The eschatological line in 50a is repeated from 42a (see 8:12).

(l) Conclusion (13:51–52)

Matthew has already used Mk's concluding formula (13:34–35), but he has placed these verses, peculiar to himself, at the end of his collection. 52. *every scribe:* The saying of v. 52 need have had no reference to the parables in its original context. The question in v. 51 concerns the "understanding" of the parables; see 13:19, where the same word is added by Matthew. The question may be composed to introduce the saying. There are no references in the NT to Christian scribes; but it has to be assumed that the members of the primitive Christian community included some scribes. Many commentators think that "Matthew" himself was such a Christian scribe. The saying is a restatement in a different form of the principle of the relations of the Law and the Gospel (5:17–20). The scribe who has become a disciple will employ both the old, the Law and the Prophets, and the new, the Gospel. Neither is sufficient without the other; for the Gospel is the fullness of the Law.

Chapter 5

Book Four

The Formation of the Disciples (13:53—18:35)

(A) Narrative Section: Various Episodes Preceding the Journey to Jerusalem (13:53—17:27)

(a) Rejection at Nazareth (13:53-58)

THE PARABLE DISCOURSE IN Mk is followed by 4:35–5:43; Matthew has used this material in 8:23–34 and 9:18–26. In both Mk and Mt the Nazareth episode forms a climax of the Galilean ministry and the rejection of Jesus. Matthew's revisions and omissions are significant. Jesus is called "the son of the carpenter" and not "the carpenter"; Matthew may have wished to raise Jesus above the actual practice of a trade. It is quite strange that in neither Mk nor Mt is the usual patronymic employed, which would be Jesus *bar*-Joseph; indeed, in Mk he is called the son of Mary, a designation that is extremely suggestive. It appears that in Nazareth it was known that Jesus was not the carnal son of Joseph, with all the implications that would be attached to this designation. 55. The kinsmen of Jesus mentioned in general in 12:46–50 are here named; it is impossible to identify them positively with others in the NT who bear these names, and the mss. are not uniform in the reading of the names. It is clear that they were never persons of importance in the primitive Jerusalem community. 57. Where Mk says Jesus "could" not work miracles, Mt says he "did" not; the phrase in Mk is harsh, but it is in agreement with the general conception of the Gospels of the miracle as a response to faith. The saying about the prophet who has no honor in his own country is found also in Jn 4:44. Mk's note of the amazement of Jesus at the unbelief of the Nazarenes is reduced in Mt to "because of their unbelief"; this amazement is an emotional response of Jesus of the type that Mt usually omits.

The incident is not only climactic in the Galilean ministry, it also summarizes the rejection of Jesus as a whole. The response of the Nazarenes was, "We know him, and therefore he cannot be anything out of the ordinary." In a proper sense the entire Jewish community could say this. The incident illustrates the saying in 10:34–36.

(b) Herod Hears of Jesus (14:1–2)

This Herod is Herod Antipas, son of Herod the Great and Malthace. After the death of Herod the Great in 4 BC Antipas received Galilee and Perea as his portion of Herod's kingdom according to Herod's will, ratified by Augustus. Mt reports only one of the various bits of gossip current about Jesus (Mk 6:15). **2. this is John the Baptist**: On the assumption that the words attributed to Herod bear some resemblance to what he said, it seems unlikely that they express a superstitious fear. John had worked no wonders, but one risen from the dead would be full of power. The burden of the remark is, "Here is another John the Baptist"—who may expect the same treatment as the first. Herod no doubt shared the common superstitious belief in miraculous power; but this would not prevent him from executing the wonder-worker if Jesus threatened to be another moral prophet as explicit as John had been [→ Chapter 5: (A) Narrative Section: (c) The Execution of John the Baptist].

(c) The Execution of John the Baptist (14:3–12)

In both Mk (6:17–29) and Mt this incident is strangely parenthetical, inserted almost as an afterthought to explain the words of Herod. Matthew has abbreviated Mk very sharply. **5.** The desire to kill John has been transferred from Herodias to Herod, and Herod's fear has been transferred from John to the crowd; and there is no mention of Herod's willingness to hear John. These alterations have the result of making Herod look still blacker. **8.** The exchange between the daughter and the mother in Mk 6:24 is omitted,

Book Four: The Formation of the Disciples (13:53—18:35)

probably to make the narrative run faster. 12. *they went and told Jesus*: This is a Matthaean addition, which not only establishes a clearer connection between the death of John and the departure of Jesus from Galilee, Herod's territory, but also makes Jesus more explicitly the successor of John.

According to Josephus (*Ant.* 18.5,2 § 116–19), the scene of the murder was the palace-fortress of Machaerus. He also informs us that the name of the daughter was Salome. According to Josephus, the scandal was less in the degree of kinship than in the open adultery that preceded the divorces. The execution of John was so barbarous and so lawless that a number of historians have questioned the historical character of the details. But the incident is quite in accord with the nature of the house of Herod as it is described by Josephus, our only witness—and, it must be confessed, a deeply prejudiced witness.

(d) The Feeding of Five Thousand (14:13–21)

Mt connects this incident with the killing of John the Baptist and the withdrawal of Jesus from Galilee. Mk associates it with the return of the Twelve from their mission and a withdrawal into solitude for rest. The scene is not clear in any of the three Syn. 13. *a desert place*: It is not identified, nor can it be said with certainty that it was on the E shore of the Sea of Galilee. However, it lay near enough to villages to make possible the purchase of food; consequently the locale is not "the desert" in the technical sense of the term. *from the cities*: The names of the cities from which the crowds followed Jesus are not given, but one has to assume that the cities on the shore of the Sea of Galilee are meant. 14. *healed their sick*: Contrast Mk (6:30) which speaks of teaching. 15. It is unlikely that very many of the crowd would leave home for a day's journey without carrying some food; the modern Palestinian peasant would not be so improvident. 17. *only five loaves and two fish*: The amount mentioned would not even suffice for Jesus and the Twelve. 19. The ceremonial with which Jesus blesses and distributes the food anticipates the Last Supper (26:26). 20. The Twelve hand out the food and collect the fragments, one basket for each. Mt heightens the number of the people: uncounted women and children besides 5000 men, who were mentioned in Mk 6:44. The number is very probably exaggerated, and it is not the result of a head count in any case; oral tradition tends to raise such figures.

The usual note of wonder that follows miracles is not mentioned here. The incident is related less for the element of the miraculous than as a symbol and an anticipation of the Eucharist and of the Messianic banquet (see 8:11–12). The association with the Eucharist is more explicit in Jn 6, where the multiplication of the loaves is followed by John's Eucharistic discourse. It is a Messianic sign and symbol that will find its fulfillment in the true Messianic banquet, the Eucharist.

Matthew has abbreviated here less sharply than elsewhere; but his abbreviations, achieved by the omission of some details and dialogue, have the effect of heightening the symbolic significance of the incident. The exception to this is his omission of Mk 6:39–40.

(e) Jesus Walks on the Water (14:22–33)

The geography remains vague; there are no "mountains" in the immediate vicinity of the lake to which Jesus could retire, but the word could be used loosely. 23. *to pray:* This is one of the few occasions when Jesus retires to pray alone (see 26:36–46). 24. *many stadia off:* Where Mk says that the boat was in the middle of the sea, Mt particularizes with "many stadia"; the *stadion* was about 600 ft. 25. *the fourth watch:* The last watch of the night, the period of about three hours before dawn. 26. *a ghost:* This is the usual meaning of *phantasma*. In Mk the wind stops, and the disciples were astonished; but Mt, as usual, omits Mk's note that the disciples were still without understanding. Mt replaces this by a very explicit confession that not only anticipates 16:16, but comes near to making 16:16–18 meaningless.

The incident is so singular in the Syn narrative that many commentators propose that in its original context it belongs after the resurrection of Jesus. Whether this was the original context or not—and it seems probable that it was—the story, like the preceding story, has a symbolic significance. This chapter begins that portion of Mt that is called the ecclesiastical portion. The disciples in the boat represent, in a not too subtle way, the Church, from which Jesus is never far even when the situation is threatening and he is invisible.

28. *on the water:* Mt alone adds the incident of Peter's attempt to walk on the water. This addition increases the symbolic significance of the story. Peter emerges into prominence in Mt's Book Four. His special position in the Twelve is clearly affirmed; here it is suggested that Peter has responsibilities not shared by the others. If he is to meet these responsibilities, he

must have faith. The faith of Peter is also a prominent theme in the story of the confession of Peter (16:13–23).

(f) Healings (14:34–36)

Matthew has made a summary of Mk (6:53–56); adhering to Mk's order of events, but abbreviating the material by the omission of graphic details. 34. *Gennesaret:* The plain at the NW shore of the Sea of Galilee, mentioned also by Josephus and regarded as a fertile and salubrious territory. 36. On healing by the touch of the tassel, see 9:20.

(g) Exterior and Interior Cleanliness (15:1–20)

This is a controversy-story concluding in a saying and its explanation. Matthew has rewritten Mk, with his expansions outbalancing his abbreviations. He omits Mk 7:2–4, an explanation of Jewish ablutions, and rearranges Mk 7:8–13 so that these lines begin the response of Jesus. 2. *the tradition of the elders:* The question is about tradition, and not about the Law. In rabbinical interpretation the traditions of the elders ranked only beneath the Law itself as a source of obligation. *wash their hands:* This particular tradition was based on a rigorous interpretation of Lv 15:11. Things that "defiled the hands" need not be articles that were technically unclean; the holy—for example, the text of the Bible—also defiled the hands, which should be washed after handling the text. 3. *he answered them:* The question is not answered directly, but by a charge: The disciples ignore the traditions, but the scribes and Pharisees nullify the Law (quoted from Ex 20:9; Dt 5:16; Ex 20:12, very nearly according to the LXX). 5. *an offering to God:* The practice to which Jesus obscurely alludes permitted the son to vow to give to the Temple the resources by which he might support his parents. This gave him the use of the resources, but the vow forbade him to convert the property to profane uses (see J. A. Fitzmyer, *JBL* 78 [1959] 60–65; J. Bligh, *HeythJ* 5[1964] 192–93). 6. *for the sake of your tradition:* The force of the example is that in this instance the traditions of the elders nullify the Law; and the implicit conclusion is that the traditions impose no obligation. 7. *well did Isaiah prophesy of you:* The attitude of the Pharisees is illustrated from Is 29:13, quoted according to the LXX, and not the MT.

10. The saying (pronounced to "the crowd") terminates the controversy; here the question concerning ablutions is answered. But the answer

goes beyond the tradition of the elders; as in the Sermon on the Mount, Jesus restates the Law, which clearly enumerates the types of unclean food (Lv 11; 17:10–16). The saying is actually an annulment rather than a restatement. 11. The controversy about the dietary laws in the primitive Christian community is frequently echoed both in Acts and in the epistles; and it is thought by many commentators that it is also reflected here. The position that is taken in Mt is also taken in the story of the vision of Peter (Acts 10:9–16; 11:1–10). In Acts, however, the principle is extended to apply by an allegorical interpretation to the admission of Gentiles to the Church. The connection is loose; but the controversy shows that the dietary laws could have become a major obstacle to the admission of Gentiles to the Church. The controversy, however, does not begin with a question about unclean foods but about ablutions; the saying is general, covering uncleanness that might be contracted by handling unclean objects and unclean foods. Matthew has abbreviated the saying with no loss of clarity. *profanes:* There is a play on the word "profane" (lit., "to make common"), which is explained in vv. 18–19.

12–14. Matthew has expanded by the addition of these verses, including the saying in 14, which comes from Q (see Lk 6:39). The expansion is pointed; the question of Pharisaic scandal is briefly handled by the saying in v. 13. Those who take scandal at the teaching of Jesus are not planted by the Father. 15. The question is proposed by the disciples in Mk, by Peter in Mt (see comment on 14:28–31). The saying is called a "parable," which means a saying with a hidden meaning, not merely a short story. 16. The disciples cannot understand the saying because it is so explicitly contrary to the prescriptions of the Law. Here Matthew, contrary to his usual practice, retains Mk's words about the failure of the disciples to understand. It may not be fanciful to think that he retains the saying here because the issue involved is the relation of Jesus to the Law, in particular his competence to interpret and even to annul the Law. The Jewish Christian who does not grasp this is indeed obtuse. 17. *whatever goes into the mouth:* The explanation of the saying is one of the most earthy passages of the Gospels, but the earthiness only adds to the earnestness of the passage. 18. *profanes:* Here the play on words is explained. Legal "cleanliness" is nothing, for all that man eats ultimately issues in the height of uncleanliness. This is irrelevant to morality. True cleanliness or uncleanness is determined from the heart. Actually not all the things mentioned proceed from the mouth; but in biblical idiom the mouth is the channel through which the heart externalizes

BOOK FOUR: THE FORMATION OF THE DISCIPLES (13:53—18:35)

itself, and the line between "word" and "deed" is thin. 19. Here Matthew has altered Mk 7:19 in a peculiar way; with the exception of "wicked plans," he enumerates the vices that are forbidden in the Decalogue. The wicked plans of the heart lie at the root of the crimes men commit. 20. *these are what profane a man:* The concluding verse returns to the subject with which the controversy began. The discussion has ranged widely to reach this answer; and it is probable that not only Matthew but Mark also has related a construction formed from several sayings.

(h) The Canaanite Woman (15:21–28)

Just as the vision of Peter is associated with the Gentile mission in Acts 10–11, so here the controversy over cleanliness and the annulment of the dietary laws is followed by one of the rare encounters of Jesus with Gentiles. The story should be compared with the healing of the centurion's slave (8:5–13). 21. *to the district of Tyre and Sidon:* That is, in southern Phoenicia. In Mk it is not clear whether Jesus left the territory of Galilee, but the implication is that he did. Mt puts him near Gentile territory but not in it; the woman "comes out." Mt's addition sharpens the point that Jesus never left Jewish territory. 22. *a Canaanite woman:* The woman is called a Syro-Phoenician in Mk, a Canaanite in Mt; both of these gentilic names occur only here in the NT. The name Canaanite suggests the OT use of the name; there, particularly in the deuteronomic and postdeuteronomic literature, the Canaanites become the sinful race that embodies all that is wicked and godless, the race that is to be exterminated. Matthew's choice of this word reflects the OT background. Contrary to what we usually find, Matthew's account is longer; and the expansions suit his general theme and purpose so well that no special source need be postulated. *Son of David:* In Mt the woman gives Jesus the Messianic title; this is highly improbable in the speech of an uninformed Gentile, but it illustrates the readiness of the Gentiles to confess the messiahship the Jews denied. 23. Mt adds to Mk the intercession of the disciples; "dismiss" here means to dismiss by granting the petition. *to the lost sheep of . . . Israel:* Mt also adds these words of Jesus; effectively they are all explanation of the proverb in v. 26, which no doubt sounded as harsh to Hellenistic readers of the Gospels as it does to modern commentators, many of whom think that it cannot be an authentic saying of Jesus. The restriction of the mission of Jesus to the Jews is clear in the entire NT, but rarely is it as explicit as here (see comment on 10:6).

The affirmation in this context heightens the difference between the believing Gentile, to whom Jesus has no mission and to whom he denies any relationship, and the unbelieving Jews. The proverb is less harsh in a Near Eastern context than it would be to us, but it is not gentle. The dialogue is an instance of the kind of wit that was and is admired in the Near East, the same wit that is called wisdom in the OT; it is the ability to match riddle with riddle, to cap one wise saying with another, to match insult with insult, or—as here—to turn the insult into a commitment. There is nothing unrealistic about the exchange at all; Jesus would not have been a genuine Palestinian if he had not occasionally engaged in a duel of wit. The scene is much more a scene of peasant good humor than it is of solemn theological debate. 28. Mark appreciates the tone when he has Jesus tell the woman that the favor is granted because of her saying. Matthew introduces the more solemn praise of her faith, the same theme that is illustrated in the healing of the slave of the centurion (8:13).

The story is not really a miracle story, nor can it be called a saying-story; it is the saying of the woman, not the miracle or the saying of Jesus, that is the climax of the episode. In this respect the story is singular. It is no doubt composed in the light of the problems of admission of Gentiles to the Church, but it is not composed entirely for this point. The story does not assert that Jesus did recommend a mission to the Gentiles; it does assert that he did not refuse faith wherever he found it.

(i) The Healing of the Sick (15:29–31)

Mt omits the geographical details of Mk (7:31–37), which show a remarkable misunderstanding of Palestinian geography. Matthew's geography is usually no more precise, but he probably found Mk unintelligible. The remarkable feature of this passage is that Matthew turns a single cure into a summary statement of several cures. It is possible that he preferred not to relate a cure that was accomplished through the use of touch and spittle; but it was also possible for him to omit these details and describe the cure by the use of a word. It is also remarkable that the praise of Jesus (Mk 7:37) is reduced to the colorless statement that they glorified the God of Israel, although the praise is actually more suitable to Mt's summary than it is to the single incident narrated in Mk. The purpose of the summary in Mt seems to be to create a transition between the story of the Canaanite woman and the feeding of the 4000; this episode explains how the crowd came to be present in a remote and unpopulated area, "the hill country."

(j) The Feeding of Four Thousand (15:32–39)

Of this passage one can say that if it is not a duplicate of the feeding of the 5000 (14:13–21), then there are no doublets anywhere in the Bible—or indeed in all literature. The variations are neither numerous nor significant: the presence of the crowd for three days; the initiative taken by Jesus; the number of loaves; the number of baskets of fragments; the number of persons (and here, as in the feeding of the 5000, Mt is careful to note that the number counts only the men). The common points are numerous: the motive of Jesus is expressly said to be compassion; the crowd is in a remote uninhabited place; the people recline on the ground; the Eucharistic formula is used; the scene is near the lake, and the miracle is followed by a trip in a boat. The terminus of the trip is Magadan in Mt, Dalmanutha in Mk. Neither name occurs elsewhere and neither can be identified.

The existence of the doublet can be explained only by the assumption that the variations occurred in the sources of Mark, and that they had been so well developed by the time they reached him that the two accounts could be taken as narratives of two different incidents. The presence of doublets is not uncommon in Mt, as we have noticed several times; but doublets are rare in Mk. That this story should have given rise to variant forms so early may indicate that it was very often told; and this in turn suggests that the connection of the story with the Eucharistic rite was present from the beginning.

(k) Signs and Times (16:1–4)

Matthew here repeats what he has already used in 12:38–39. **1.** *a sign:* See comment on 12:38. **2b–3.** These words are missing in many important mss., and many critics regard them as a secondary gloss. Lk 12:54–55 is not an exact parallel, and this suggests that the substratum in Q was different from both Lk and Mt. It is easier to suppose that weather phenomena, which are peculiar to most regions anyway, would be altered when the Gospel traditions were retold in another climate. The Mediterranean climate is generally uniform throughout the whole basin; but Palestine has its own peculiarities. The redness of the sky comes from atmospheric dust that accumulates during the dry summer months. The sign can only refer to the beginning of the rainy season. The type of cloudiness that indicates the first rain of the winter is such that once observed, it is not likely to be misconstrued. The Arabs say "Rain tomorrow" (predicting a day in advance of the time indicated in 16:3) with an assurance that the foreigner will do well to respect. 3. *the times:* The Messianic times (Gk *kairoi*). 4. See comment on 12:38.

(l) Leaven (16:5-12)

Mt's abbreviations of Mk (8:14-21) are significant. Lk (12:1) gives the saying and the situation in a much more compressed form, but adds an explicit note that the leaven of the Pharisees is hypocrisy. This is not clearly the force of the saying, and it is quite possible that the original context is not preserved. The most obvious meaning of the figure is the teaching of the Pharisees and Sadducees; but Mk has Pharisees and Herod, and Herod cannot be considered a teacher. Mt's change of "Herod" to "Sadducees" may have been made to suggest the idea of teaching. 7. *we brought no bread:* The disciples failed completely to grasp the figure and thought that it referred to their own forgetfulness; this elicits an extremely sharp rebuke from Jesus, which is considerably softened in Mt by the omission of Mk 8:17b-18. 9-10. The direction of the story is then turned from the Pharisees and the Sadducees to a lesson of faith; Jesus has proved that he can provide for their needs. This is doubtfully a part of the original saying-story. 12. *then they understood:* Mt still further softens the rebuke of the disciples by adding that they understood after the rebuke and gives the explanation of the figure as teaching; Mk leaves the rebuke hanging in the air.

The episode is placed on "the opposite side" by Mt, in the boat by Mk. This journey takes Jesus and the disciples to a point from which they can travel to Caesarea Philippi, the scene of the next incident. Mt omits the healing of the blind man of Bethsaida (Mk 8:22-26).

(m) The Confession of Peter (16:13-23)

The scene of this conversation is the neighborhood of Caesarea Philippi, the modern Baniyas, a little over 20 mi. N of the Sea of Galilee near the sources of the Jordan. The city was founded by Philip the tetrarch, brother of Herod Antipas; it was an entirely Gentile community. The variations of Mt from Mk here are some of the most interesting in the entire Gospel. The

Book Four: The Formation of the Disciples (13:53—18:35)

question of Jesus concerns the Son of Man where Mk has "me"; Son of Man is usually understood to be a Messianic title, but suggestive rather than explicit. To the answers John the Baptist (see 14:2) and Elijah, or another of the prophets, Mt adds Jeremiah. The belief in the return of Elijah was derived from Mal 3:23-24; see Sir 48:10; Mt 17:3,10-13. The addition of Jeremiah may not be unrelated to the belief expressed in 2 Mc 15:13-16. The question is turned directly to the disciples; and the construction of the passage leaves no doubt that it is a challenge. "Simon Peter" answers for all with a profession that Jesus is the Messiah; Mt alone adds "the son of the living God." This additional title, which goes beyond the confession of messiahship, very probably reflects the more developed faith of the primitive Christian community; Mk has preserved the original saying. By speaking of the more developed faith of the community we do not imply that the community had a full understanding of the sonship of Jesus; but they professed their belief in the entirely unique relationship of Jesus with the Father (see 11:27; T. de Kruijf, *Der Sohn des lebendigen Gottes* [AnalBib 16; Rome, 1962]).

Verses 17-20 have no parallel in Mk and Lk; and there can be no explanation of this omission except that Mk and Lk did not have the words. Some writers have suggested that the verses have been removed from their original context, which was post-resurrectional, and that they can be compared to Jn 21:15-19, in which Peter is given a peculiar position in a postresurrectional narrative (see R. E. Brown, *CBQ* 23 [1961] 159). The arguments for this hypothesis are not convincing; and in the context of Mt the words are spoken to Simon Peter in response to his faith. 17. *but my Father who is in heaven*: Simon's confession of messiahship is attributed to divine revelation; it could not come from his own perception or from the instruction of others. This itself is an interesting testimony to the way in which the primitive Church thought that the messiahship of Jesus was recognized. 18. *you are Peter*: Jesus then gives Simon bar-Jona a new name and a commission, which is set forth in the most vigorously discussed passage of the Gospel. (For a full discussion see O. Cullmann, *Peter* [rev. ed.; London, 1962]; O. Karrer, *Peter and the Church* [QD 8; N.Y., 1963].) Simon gets the name by which he is usually known in the NT; and those who doubt that Jesus spoke these words forget that the NT has no other passage in which the change of name is explained. This does not imply that Mt has preserved "the very words" of Jesus; this can rarely be said of any passage in the Gospels. "Peter" comes from the Gk *petros*, the masculinized form of the fem. noun *petra*, "rock," which represents the Aram *kēphā*. The Aram name occurs once in the Grecized form *Kēphas* in Jn 1:43; 1 Cor 1:12; 3:22; 9:5; 15:5; Gal 1:18; 2:9,11,14; Paul uses *Petros* only in Gal 2:7,8. *upon this rock:* That Peter is the rock upon which the *ekklēsia* is to be built is clear; but in what sense he is the foundation is not. The word *ekklēsia* is used only here and 18:17 in all the Gospels; and it is highly doubtful that Jesus himself used the word, which becomes the common designation of the Christian community in the epistles. Whether Jesus used the word has nothing to do with whether the primitive community understood him correctly when they believed that he intended to form an enduring community.

In the context the reason why Peter is called the rock is the faith that he has just shown in his confession. He has made vocal the faith of the disciples; and it is upon faith in Jesus as the Messiah that the group Jesus has formed will endure. Peter is the speaker and the example of this faith. As long as this faith endures, "the gates of Sheol" will not have power over the group. *gates of hell:* The common translation is misleading; the phrase means not the powers of evil but the power of death; for Sheol is the biblical abode of the dead.

19. *the keys of the kingdom:* The conferring of the keys is a clear statement of a position of leadership and authority. The phrase echoes Is 22:22, in which Shebna receives the keys of the royal palace. The key was the symbol of the office of master of the palace, the highest of the officers of the Israelite court; and Peter is thus declared master of the palace in the *ekklēsia*. The phrase "kingdom of heaven" is used here not in its usual sense of reign, but of the community established by the reign, practically synonymous with *ekklēsia*. *whatever you bind . . . you loose:* The meaning of the office conferred is further specified in the conferring of the power to bind and loose. This phrase is obscure; it has no background in biblical language, and in rabbinical Judaism it signifies rabbinical decisions; to bind is to give a decision that imposes an obligation, and to loose is to give a decision that removes an obligation. If this is the sense in which the phrase is used, it does not mean that Peter becomes chief rabbi in the Church; for his decisions are accepted in heaven. The same phrase is used of the Church as a whole in 18:18; there it refers to expulsion from the Church. The phrase certainly signifies the exercise of authority; but the nature and use of the authority are not specified. That Peter had a special position in the early Church is clear from other passages in the NT; see Lk 22:31–32; Jn 21:15–19; Acts 1–12.

BOOK FOUR: THE FORMATION OF THE DISCIPLES (13:53—18:35)

20. By the insertion of vv. 17–19 Matthew has taken some of the point from Mk's arrangement; but he retains what Mk has. In Mk the question leads from a confession of messiahship to an instruction in the suffering of the Messiah. This is a crisis in the Gospel narrative; for the idea was entirely foreign to the Judaism of NT times. *the Christ [or the Messiah]*: The confession is followed by a prohibition to reveal the messiahship; Mt makes this explicit by the addition of "the Messiah." If the faith of the disciples is firm, they are ready for this instruction. 21. Where Mk has "the Son of Man" (9:31) Mt has "him," with "Jesus Messiah" as subject. Mt also adds Jerusalem as the place of the events. The Gospels describe very briefly what must have been one of the great disillusionments in the minds of the disciples; but the early disillusionment had long been forgotten. 22. *Peter . . . started to reproach him*: Not forgotten, however, was the response of Peter; Lk spares Peter by omitting the passage. Mk mentions that Jesus saw the disciples present before he answered Peter, which adds to the humiliation of Peter. 23. *You are a scandal to me*: Mt's additional phrase is no less humiliating. *scandal*: See comment on 11:6. Peter is called an obstacle, an adversary, an enemy; and the occurrence of this verse immediately after the confession and the conferring of the name and the commission is certainly striking. Contrary to his usual practice, Matthew makes the exchange more vivid by quoting Peter's words directly. The revelation of Jesus as Messiah was more easily received than the revelation that the Messiah must suffer, die, and rise.

(n) Discipleship (16:24–28)

This passage contains a collection of sayings brought together by Mk; but Mt does not follow Mk closely. The connection with the prediction of the passion is established by Mk; the word "cross" does not appear in the prediction, but the association is obvious. Mt omits Mk's crowds (8:34); the scene of Caesarea Philippi made this detail unlikely. Matthew has used the sayings of 16:24–25 earlier (see 10:38–39); the form in which they are set here is almost identical with Mk. 24. *let him deny himself*: The "denial of self" does not mean the renunciation of some optional good, as the phrase is commonly used; it means the affirmation that the self is nothing, that it has no claims and no values. The phrase is echoed in Paul's saying that Jesus emptied himself (Phil 2:7). *take up his cross*: Lk adds "daily," thus giving the phrase a more clearly metaphorical turn; but the original phrase very probably echoes the martyrdoms of the primitive Church. 26. *self*: See comment on 10:39. This translation does not take away the implicit affirmation of the verse that the true and lasting value of the person transcends the conditions of the present existence. The whole world is not a sufficient recompense for the surrender of the self (*psychē*) to prolong one's earthly life. Matthew omits Mk 8:37-38; he has already used this saying (in a variant form) in 10:33, although there are many other instances where he uses the same saying twice. 27. *the Son of Man is to come . . .* : Because of the omission Mk 8:38b had to be recast; and the allusion to the judgment becomes more general in Mt. The judgment is a coming in glory with the angels; see 24:29-31. The function of the angels in the judgment appears in the parables of the reign; see 13:36-50. The judgment is described in terms drawn from Ps 62:13. The allusion to the glory is a catchword by which 16:28 is attached to the preceding passage. 28. The saying was paradoxical enough even in the primitive Church to be preserved in three forms (Mk, "the Reign of God coming in power"; Mt, "the Son of Man coming in his Reign"; Lk, "the Reign of God"). It has been remarked on 10:23 that such sayings are inexplicable on the hypothesis that they indicate that the parousia is near. Like 10:23b, this saying must have been understood to refer to another display of judgment in power, and this display was most probably the catastrophic destruction of Jerusalem in AD 70.

(o) The Transfiguration (17:1-8)

Matthew has condensed Mk (9:2-8) in some parts of this narrative and expanded it in others. In 17:2 he has added a glow to the countenance of Jesus where Mk speaks of the whiteness of his garments, but he has omitted Mk's allusion to the fuller. In 17:4 he has omitted Mk's reference to Peter's ignorance and the fear of the disciples; but in 17:6-7 he has added a deeper note of fear and reverence and presents Jesus himself as arousing the disciples. The effect of these modifications is to heighten the majesty and the mystery of the experience and to remove, as he often does, suggestions that the disciples did not understand what was happening.

1. *mountain*: Traditionally understood as Mt. Tabor in the plain of Esdraelon; but since Tabor is not notably high, Mt. Hermon north of Caesarea Philippi (over 9000 ft. high) has been suggested. It is far more probable that this mountain, like the mountain of the sermon (5:1) has no geographical location. It is the symbolic mountain on which the events of Sinai are

Book Four: The Formation of the Disciples (13:53—18:35)

re-enacted in the life of the new Moses. *Peter, James, and John:* The three who accompany Jesus are the same three who are his exclusive companions in other events (26:37; Mk 5:37, not followed by Mt). *after six days:* The interval is thought to echo Ex 24:16, but the parallel is not close; the themes of the episode, however, do echo the Sinai narrative. 2. *was transfigured:* The luminous clarity with which Jesus is surrounded recalls the brightness of the face of Moses after the Sinai revelation (Ex 34:29–35), which made it necessary for Moses to veil his face; this feature is added in Mt. 3. *Moses and Elijah:* They are symbolic figures, representing respectively the Law and the Prophets. These two words are used to designate the entire collection of OT books, and thus the fullness of the revelation of God to Israel. Jesus joins the two as the fulfillment of the Law and the Prophets (see 5:17). 4. *I will make three booths:* The remark of Peter alludes to the Feast of Tabernacles. This feast commemorated the sojourn of the Israelites on Mt. Sinai while they received the revelation of the Law through Moses. But this is not the revelation of another Law; a greater reality is manifested here. The external symbol is again derived from the Sinai narratives. 5. *a bright cloud:* The luminous cloud is the Shekinah, the symbol of the presence of God. In a cloud God comes to declare the Law to Moses (Ex 19:9; 24:15–16), and he speaks from the cloud as he does here. *my beloved Son:* The words spoken are a revelation of the sonship of Jesus; Mt repeats the formula of the baptism (3:17), with the addition of Mk's phrase, "Hear him." Jesus is the son and the revealer. The formula very probably echoes the Servant passage of Is 42:1 (see 3:17). 7. The suggestion that the disciples were asleep is much clearer in Lk; this extraordinary experience was more easily conceived as a dream-vision.

The transfiguration has no parallel in the Syn except the Baptism Narrative; and for this reason some scholars have suggested that it is a postresurrection narrative transferred to this point. This opinion is not accepted by the vast majority of commentators. The external features of the narrative, we have noticed, are derived from the Exodus narratives rather than from the resurrection narratives. The heavily symbolic character of the story indicates that this story, like the story of Jesus' baptism, is more theological than historical in character. The narrative must rest upon a mystical experience of the disciples, but the experience is described in symbolic imagery in such a way that the experience itself is impossible to reconstruct. The course of events in the Gospels compels us to suppose that the fullness of perception into the reality of Jesus that the transfiguration suggests was not possessed by the disciples until after the resurrection. The position of the narrative here—after the confession of Peter and the prediction of the passion—makes it a reaffirmation of the messiahship of Jesus and of the Messianic glory in which he will be revealed. He is no less Messiah when his Messianic glory is hidden in the incarnation and the passion.

(p) The Coming of Elijah (17:9–13)

The precept of Jesus not to reveal "the vision" (this word occurs in Mt but not in Mk) is a part of Mk's Messianic secret, which Matthew has retained. But he has not retained Mk's observation that the disciples did not understand what was meant by the resurrection; as usual, he omits passages that show their lack of insight.

The context of the preceding chapter and of the transfiguration has been Messianic; and the question of the disciples about the coming of Elijah supposes that Elijah would return as a messianic precursor (see 16:14). If Jesus is Messiah, what has happened to this sign of the Messianic age? 12. *has already come:* The answer of Jesus is that Elijah has come (alluding to Mal 3:23, LXX) but has not been recognized (added by Mt). As "Elijah" was treated by men according to their will, so shall the Son of Man suffer; Mt transfers this allusion to the passion from its position in Mk, and thus secures a parallel between the death of John the Baptist and the death of Jesus. 13. Mt adds explicitly that "Elijah" was John the Baptist. It seems very probable that this dialogue is constructed in the light of the controversies between Christians and Jews in the primitive Church. Jews would have asked about the traditional Messianic signs, and Jewish Christians were obliged to meet their request.

(q) The Healing of an Epileptic Child (17:14–21)

This exorcism story, one of the most vivid in Mk (9:14–29) has been condensed in Mt to less than half, including the expansion in 17:20. The healing-story issues in a saying, but Matthew has changed the saying (see comment on 17:20). 14. *to the crowd:* The presence of the crowd at the foot of the mountain is introduced in Mt without any of Mk's explanation; but the geography, as we have noticed, is more ideal than real, and the conjunction of the incidents seems to be artificial. Nor does Mt retain the dispute between the disciples and the scribes, which in Mk has no object.

Book Four: The Formation of the Disciples (13:53—18:35)

15. *an epileptic:* The nature of the ailment, which in Mk is demonic possession, is called "lunacy" in Mt; in the ancient world attacks of mental disease were attributed to the phases of the moon. But there is no doubt that the symptoms of epilepsy are described. Mt omits the details given in Mk concerning the symptoms, the attack the child suffers when he is brought to Jesus, and the dialogue of Jesus with the father concerning faith; but Mt does retain the theme of faith and places it in the concluding saying. 17. The apostrophe to the "unbelieving and perverse generation" (possibly in Mt an allusion to Dt 32:5) is difficult to explain; it seems to refer directly not to the father, nor to the crowd, but rather to the disciples who have failed in the use of the power that Jesus communicated to them (see 10:8; 17:19–20). 18. *rebuked him:* Mk's account of the healing suggests an unusual struggle and resistance; Mt reduces the healing to a bare minimum.

20. Mk's answer to the question of the disciples, "This kind is expelled only by prayer," was too difficult for both Matthew and Luke. Matthew has substituted a saying on faith adapted from Mk 11:22–23, which he uses again in 21:21. The failure of the disciples is due not to lack of prayer but to lack of faith; it is doubtful that any real difference between the two is intended. The saying on faith introduces a theme that is both more familiar and easier to grasp. The saying is cast in a hyperbole that contrasts the smallness of the grain of mustard (see 13:31–32) with the mountain. The explanation removes any idea that the power communicated to the disciples has any essential limitations; it was simply a lapse in that which is the basis of all the power that Jesus communicates. 21. A number of mss. add this verse based on Mk 9:29 with the addition of "fasting" to "prayer"; but it does not belong to the critical text.

(r) The Second Prediction of the Passion (17:22–23)

The "gathering" of the disciples is for the journey to Jerusalem (19:1). Mt omits Mk's notice (9:30) that Jesus traveled without wishing to be known, as well as Mk's statement that the prediction of the passion was the object of the teaching of Jesus. This prediction of the passion has fewer details than the other predictions; the slayers are simply "men," and the only detail added is that Jesus will be betrayed. Mk's frank statement that the disciples did not understand the saying is altered by Matthew, according to his practice, to a statement that they were grieved.

(s) The Temple Tax (17:24–27)

This episode is peculiar to Mt; and it is another in this series of texts that raises Peter to a special position in the company of the disciples (see 16:13–23). But the position of Peter is not the main point of the story. According to Ex 30:13–15 (a late passage), each adult male Jew owed a half-shekel annual tax for the maintenance of the Temple. The payment here is made in Attic coinage; the double drachma was equal to a half-shekel and the stater, four drachmas, was payment for two persons. 24. *Peter:* Aware of Jesus' habitual observance of the Law joined with affirmation of his independence of the Law, Peter assured the collectors that Jesus paid the tax. This passage gives occasion for a saying. 25. *their sons:* The "sons" from whom the kings of the earth do not collect taxes are the subjects of the king as opposed to residents who are citizens of other countries. Rome at this period did not tax Roman citizens; the revenues of the government were obtained by taxing allies, provinces, and satellite kingdoms. 26. Jesus claims the same freedom for himself and for his disciples; by their association with him they share to this extent in his own freedom. 27. *not to give offense:* The reason for paying the tax is purely to avoid scandal. The stater will be obtained by catching a fish. That foreign objects are often found in fish is not to the point. It is remarkable that there is no statement that the coin was actually found in this manner.

The saying and the construction of the dialogue in which it occurs seem to reflect the position of Jewish Christians in the first generation of the Church toward the Temple tax. They regarded themselves as Jews and observed the Law and the cult. But the idea of freedom was not limited to Paul and Hellenistic Christian communities. If Jewish Christians paid the Temple tax, it was to preserve the decencies and not because they lay under the obligation of the Law to pay the tax. Jesus is greater than the Temple (12:6).

(B) Discourse: The Sermon on the Church (18:1–35)

From 18:1–14 this discourse is almost entirely drawn from Mk with some additions from Q; the rest of the discourse is peculiar to Mt. The theme of the discourse is the relations between the disciples. The word *ekklēsia* occurs here for the second and last time in the Gospels. Mt arranges the sayings to fit the idea of a community with many close relations between

Book Four: The Formation of the Disciples (13:53—18:35)

the members. The discourse is not "ecclesiastical" in the sense that it speaks of the structure of the Church; no officer of the Church is mentioned, and the single allusion to pre-eminence in the Church is followed by a warning against pride of place. The discourse sets forth the spirit that should be exhibited by the members in their relations with one another. The topics are not treated in a logical and consecutive structure.

(a) Greatness in the Reign (18:1–5)

The theme of this saying appears elsewhere in the Gospel; see 20:26–27; 23:11–12. Mk (9:33–37) has combined two unrelated sayings in a single unit by the catchword "child." Matthew has rewritten Mk in such a way as to reduce the two sayings to one; but he adds the second saying of Mk in an appendix (18:5). 1. *who is the greatest*: The saying in Mk arises from a dispute among the disciples, a dispute they recognize as altogether foreign to the mind of Jesus. Mt omits this unflattering detail and has the disciples ask the question about rank directly. *reign*: Here, as in a few other passages, *basileia* is more properly translated "kingdom," referring to the community of the Church. The question is not unrelated to the position among the disciples (see 16:13–23). 2. *calling a child to him*: The answer is given by bringing the child into the group; even in the modern Near East it is rare that a group of adults gathers without at least one small child standing right behind them. 3. *unless you become . . .* : The saying is closely related to Mk 10:15 and nearly identical with Lk 18:17 (Q par.). Becoming like a child is not only a condition for greatness in the reign, it is a condition of admission. 4. *whoever humbles himself*: Mt adds the precept of lowering oneself to clarify what is meant by becoming like a child. In ancient law the child was not a person in the full legal sense. He was not only under the authority of the parents, he was their property; he had no power of self-assertion and no power of independent action. This "denial of self" (16:24) is the proper posture of those who would be "great"—that is, the bearers of authority—in the reign. 5. The saying is joined to the preceding by the catchword "child." "Child" here is possibly not meant in its literal sense, although the same idea is stated in 19:10–13; the word may designate the simple who become disciples and who already have that simplicity that Jesus states as the condition of membership. With these "little ones" Jesus identifies himself. Elsewhere those who receive the disciples receive Jesus (10:40).

(b) Scandals (18:6–9)

By a change from "child" to "little ones" the association is retained, but the little ones become more clearly the simple disciples "who believe." 6. *scandalizes:* That is, causes to stumble (see comment on 11:6). Presumably the simple are in greater danger of being misled (see 11:6). The words of Jesus are severe. *great millstone:* A millstone drawn by an ass would be notably larger than the hand millstone so frequently found in Palestinian sites and of a type still used; actually the hand millstone is large enough for the purpose, but by hyperbole probably the larger stone is meant. This is a flat circular stone that is revolved over the lower stone, of corresponding shape and size, to make meal. A favorite material is basalt, which has a high specific gravity. 7. This verse is peculiar to Mt; it is an assertion of the ineradicable malice of man, which brings woe to the world. The inevitability of the scandal, however, does not excuse the individual person who is responsible for it. 8–9. These sayings already occur in 5:29–30. Here Mt follows the text of Mk more closely, but compresses the first two of Mk's pronouncements into one. The obstacle, the object by which one is tempted to sin, may be in oneself as well as in another person. A woe cannot be pronounced upon the self, but the occasion of offense must be removed. The fact that the saying is couched in a rather intense hyperbole does not entitle interpreters to reduce it to a vague form of spiritual detachment. *eternal fire:* This and "the Gehenna of fire" are derived from Jewish literature; and the image in turn is derived from Is 66:24 (quoted by Mk 9:48, but not by Mt). "Gehenna" (Gk *geenna*) refers to the ravine S of Jerusalem (the modern Wadi er-Rababy), which in ancient times was the place where rubbish was burned. In Is the bodies of the enemies of Israel are thrown here.

The sayings on scandal are addressed to the entire group of disciples; but without any direct reference to the leaders in the Church, it is evident that the words of Jesus about the scribes and Pharisees (see v. 23) show that these words have a special reference to those in the Church who by their position of leadership are both better able and more likely to place obstacles in the way of the simple. The saying is addressed to all members; but the "little ones" are presumably mentioned in contrast to "the greater."

BOOK FOUR: THE FORMATION OF THE DISCIPLES (13:53—18:35)

(c) The Lost Sheep (18:10-14)

This parable comes from Q; but it has different forms and different applications in Mt and in Lk. Lk gives the parable as the answer of Jesus to the charge that he fraternizes with tax collectors and sinners; in Mt it illustrates the saying of 18:10 (peculiar to Mt) addressed to the disciples. 10. *little ones*: Again the simple disciples are meant, whom the "great" may be tempted to despise. But the simple have powerful friends: "their" angels. The belief that angels guard the righteous appears in the OT and very frequently in the literature of Judaism (Str-B 1, 781–83). *see the face*: A technical term that designates the prerogative of those members of a royal court who immediately attend upon the king; the phrase shows the intercessory power of the angels. 11. Some mss. add this verse taken actually from Lk 19:10.

12. The precept is reinforced by the parable of the shepherd. The shepherd can with some assurance leave the entire flock alone for a short time even in the mountains (Lk, "in the desert"); sheep are gregarious and do not readily scatter. But the one that has strayed may have fallen and must be sought out. The parable does not suggest that one person is equal in value to one hundred, but that the shepherd must not let one go because it is only one. It is the will of the Father that not even one should perish. Deliberately or not, the passage echoes the words about the watchman in Ez 33:1–9. The responsibility that Jesus takes as his own in Lk becomes the responsibility of the shepherds in the Church in Mt.

(d) Fraternal Correction (18:15-20)

This passage shows one of the ways in which the members of the Church must seek out the sheep that has wandered. To the saying about correction is added a saying about prayer (19–20). The passage is peculiar to Mt. 15. *sins against you*: Many Gk mss. (and the Vg) add the prepositional phrase "against you" (*eis se*); but it does not belong to the critical text. The duty of correction is therefore not limited to offenses that are personal. The whole point of the preceding parallel would be annulled by this reservation. Any individual member of the community should try to "gain" the offending brother, the stray sheep; and this is done privately, so that the brother is not humiliated. 16. But should he be recalcitrant, a few witnesses are to be summoned for another reproval. In the law of Dt 19:15 the evidence of a single witness is not enough for a conviction; the principle is applied here somewhat loosely. The witnesses are to add weight to the reproval, which they can only do by sharing it. 17. Failure to heed this more solemn warning demands that the process be brought before the *ekklēsia*, here the local church community. A similar procedure was used in the Qumran community (1QS 5:25—6:1; cf. H. Braun, *TRu* 28 [1962] 134-36). *as a Gentile and a tax collector:* If the offender will not accept the verdict of the Church, he must be expelled from membership. Expulsion was used by Paul against an offender at Corinth (1 Cor 5:1-5). The words of excommunication are strangely discordant with the general tone of the Gospels, in which Jesus is called a friend of sinners and tax collectors; and these classes as well as Gentiles are sometimes praised for their faith and repentance. The words are a stock phrase to designate those who were unacceptable within the Jewish community. Together with other features of the passage, they suggest that this saying was formed within the primitive Jewish Christian community. 18. *bind . . . loose:* See comment on 16:19. In this context the words clearly have the force of "condemn" or "acquit." The whole assembly of the Church has the power that is given to Peter in 16:19; and it should be noticed that the acts of the Church in Acts are always the acts of the whole Church, not of its officers. The apostolic Church was a true assembly.

19-20. The idea of assembly leads by association to the next saying. *should two of you agree:* This saying affirms the efficacy of the common prayer of the Church, but common prayer does not mean the prayer of the entire Church; even two or three form an assembly where the prayer of the Church is offered. The reason for this efficacy is that Jesus himself is present in any community of Christians, and two or three are as small a number as one can have in a community. The idea of Christian community expressed here seems to reflect a more developed conception of the Church; and the saying, like the saying that precedes it, appears to derive its form from the primitive Church.

(e) Forgiveness (18:21-22)

The saying is a development by Mt of a saying found in Q (Lk 17:4). Mt makes it an answer to a question asked by Peter. *seven times:* If account is taken of the symbolic value of the number seven, it should signify a definite but not specified number; there should be a point at which forgiveness becomes perfect, and the duty to forgive ceases if the offense continues. By the multiplication of seven by itself and ten Jesus uses another symbolic

Book Four: The Formation of the Disciples (13:53—18:35)

significance of the number and makes the number indefinite; no definite number makes forgiveness perfect. The phrase surely echoes the saying of Lamech in Gn 4:24, in which a limit is denied to the satisfaction of blood revenge. The Gospel inverts the old dispensation.

(f) The Parable of the Unmerciful Servant (18:23–25)

This parable, peculiar to Mt, is one of the sternest passages of the Gospels. It reinforces the duty of forgiveness by appealing to another motive: the forgiveness granted by man to man as a condition of forgiveness granted to man by God (see 6:15). **23.** *the reign of God:* Again, that to which the "king" is likened is rather the "kingdom," the community of the Church; the parable describes conditions in the Church. The king is an Oriental despot, and the "slave" with the immense debt is not a domestic; he is a high officer of state, a viceroy, who has the disposal of enormous funds and has defaulted in his payment of revenue. **24.** *ten thousand talents:* The value of the talent cannot be reckoned in terms of modern coinage with any degree of accuracy; the sum of 10,000 talents is intended to represent an incredibly large sum, something like the national debt of the United States falling upon a single citizen. **25.** *to be sold:* The unreal sum is matched with a very realistic and common procedure, the sale of the man and his family into slavery for debt; but the sale would not pay the debt. **26.** *imploring him:* The slave promises payment, and the king not only accepts the promise but forgives the whole debt. This generosity is contrasted with the attitude of the slave, who assaults and imprisons a fellow slave for a debt of 100 denarii, a comprehensible sum; the denarius was the daily wage of common casual labor (20:2). **34.** *until he would pay all his debt:* The king punishes the slave with torture because he has not forgiven as he was forgiven; torture does not repay the debt, and no end to the torture is possible under these conditions.

The parable illustrates the principle that details should not be allegorized. The conduct of the king is not a model by which we should learn the providence of God. The detail that is most significant is the difference in the debt owed by the merciless servant and the debt that he claims. The model is the forgiveness of God, which knows no limit; and neither should man's forgiveness. If man does not forgive, he cannot expect forgiveness; if he does not renounce his own claims, which are small, he cannot ask God to dismiss the claims against him.

Chapter 6

Book Five
Judea and Jerusalem (19:1—25:46)

THE EVENTS OF THIS book represent a very brief period; as in the preceding books, there is a narrative section and a discourse [for the treatment of ch. 23 → Introduction: (V) Outline].

(A) Narrative Section: Journey to Jerusalem and Events There (19:1—23:39)

The journey to Jerusalem is related in chs. 19–20, and the entire remainder of the Gospel covers a period of eight days from the entrance into Jerusalem to the day of the resurrection.

(a) Marriage, Divorce, and Celibacy (19:1–12)

The opening verse is Mt's standard concluding formula to the discourses. The geography, vague in Mk (10:1–12), becomes impossible in Mt; there was no "Judea across the Jordan." The phrase somewhat clumsily designates a journey from Galilee to Judea through eastern Palestine; this route would avoid the territory of the Samaritans. For Mk's "taught," Mt has "healed" (19:2).

    3. The discussion on marriage and divorce is a fuller treatment of the principle stated in 5:31–32. Mt adds that the Pharisees' question was posed as a "temptation." *for any cause:* The question is rephrased so that it does

not deal simply with divorce (Mk 10:2) but with divorce "for any cause"; Jesus is asked to give an opinion on the dispute between the rabbinical schools of Hillel and Shammai (Str-B 1, 303–321). Hillel permitted divorce literally "for any cause," but Shammai permitted it only for adultery. It is rather important in interpreting Mt to notice the question. Mt has transposed Mk 10:4–5 so that these verses follow 19:6. 4. *have you not read:* Jesus' answer is given in good rabbinical style by quoting the text of the Law; he appeals to Gn 1:27 and 2:24 as arguments for a permanent state of unity created by marriage. The quotations follow the LXX rather closely, but the LXX here is faithful to the MT. 6. *what God has joined:* Since this union is a work of creation and formally stated in the Law, it is the work of God, with which man may not tamper. This is an appeal to the primitive institution of marriage; Jesus goes behind the Law to creation, an argument that would not please the questioners but one they could hardly contest. 7. *why then did Moses . . . :* Their rebuttal (placed in this position by Mt) asks why the Law makes provision for divorce (Dt 24:1). The obscure allusion to "some indecency" in this verse of Dt furnished the occasion for the various interpretations of Hillel and Shammai. 8. *from the beginning it was not so:* The answer of Jesus is a candid devaluation of the Law (see 5:17–20). The law of divorce is a concession to "hardness of heart," a deviation from the original institution. Jesus then states the law as restored to its original force.

9. In Mk the statement (10:11) is given to the disciples alone, in Mt to the questioners. Mk's statement is written in the light of Roman law, which permitted either the husband or the wife to institute divorce. Mk's formula is a clear, total prohibition of divorce. Mt has in a briefer form the exception contained in 5:32 [→ Chapter 2: (B) Discourse: (c) The Law and the Gospel: (iii) Divorce]. The preceding context is completely in harmony with the interpretation that Mt's statement does not contain an exception permitting divorce for adultery. The exception would be in open contradiction with the argument on which the statement is based and would place Jesus simply on the side of the school of Shammai. This opinion could have been given without the argument that is employed.

10. *if such is the case:* Only Mt reports the disciples' reaction: They do not understand an exception permitting divorce. Their naïve reaction was that the single state is preferable to an indissoluble marriage. By association this leads to another saying, found only in Mt. Indeed celibacy can be preferable to marriage, but not for many. 12. Some live without marriage by reason of a natal defect or surgery; the state of celibacy is not always of one's

own choice. But it is also possible for one to renounce marriage because of the reign of God. The statement is extremely daring in a Jewish context, and the final phrase, "Let him take who can," shows awareness of the challenge. For what purpose is this renunciation made? Jesus does not specify; but the saying is not unrelated to the sayings that insist on renunciation (see 19:29). If the Christian vocation can divide families, it can also detach one from founding a family. The saying has no antecedent in Judaism. Continence was practiced at Qumran, but it is not clear that it was more than temporary abstinence.

(b) The Blessing of the Children (19:13–15)

In Mk (10:13–16) this episode is a saying-story; the readiness of Jesus to receive children is the occasion of the saying in Mk 10:15. But Matthew has transferred this saying to 18:3 [→ Chapter 5: (B) Discourse: (a) Greatness in the Reign]. He has made both the request of the parents and the action of Jesus more formal, even ritual, than they are in Mk; but he leaves out the embrace of the children. As usual, he omits Mk's notice that Jesus was irritated at the officiousness of the disciples. Mt's version of the incident has the same meaning as it has in Mk, even with the transfer of Mk 10:15 to another context. The main purpose is not to show the affability of Jesus—for modern readers one of the most precious traits of the Gospels. **13.** *children:* Jesus accepts the children because they are the "little ones," the simple to whom the gospel is proclaimed. The gospel was not literally proclaimed to children: but the dispositions demanded for the reception of the gospel impose upon the disciples the necessity of reducing self-importance. The lesson is the same as the lesson of 18:1–5; and the affability of Jesus toward children suits what is said of him in 11:19.

(c) The Rich Young Man (19:16–30)

This passage, the source of the evangelical counsels in Catholic tradition, contains a number of sayings of Jesus that revolve about the theme of wealth. The sayings are set within a framework of dialogue. Matthew has made some changes in Mk (10:17–31) without altering the character of the sayings. He omits Mk's vivid description of the approach of the man and changes the form of both question and answer. **16.** *Master, what good deed . . . :* Matthew omits the adjective "good" modifying "master" (Mk

Book Five: Judea and Jerusalem (19:1—25:46)

10:17) and changes the question to "What good shall I do?" This allows him to change the answer of Jesus; that Jesus should reject the title "good," and still more that he should affirm the exclusive goodness of God in such a way that he seemed to deny goodness of himself, was too difficult for Matthew to retain. *to have eternal life:* Jewish moral thinking underlies the man's question; "eternal life" has no reference to the peculiarly Christian idea of life developed in other NT books. 17. *keep the commandments:* The answer of Jesus is also couched within the scope of Jewish moral thinking; five of the ten commandments are cited, with the addition of the commandment of love of God and neighbor. This last commandment is not found in Mk (10:19); but Mk adds "Do not defraud," omitted in Mt. Curiously Mt represents Jesus as eliciting the enumeration by a Socratic question; in Mk, Jesus himself enumerates the commandments. The way to eternal life in the answer is the way of Jewish morality; there is no call to faith in Jesus nor to any new morality. This is more contrary to the proclamation that Jesus gives elsewhere in the Gospels than most commentators have noticed; and the presentation must be meant to be pedagogical. 20. *what do I still lack:* Jesus brings the man to the point where he himself asks for something more. The word "lack" is taken from the words of Jesus in Mk 10:21. Mk notes that Jesus looked on him and loved him; Matthew omits this trait, as he usually omits emotional expressions attributed to Jesus. Matthew calls the man "a youth," and this is probably derived from Mk 10:20; but the words of Mk suggest a mature man rather than a youth. 21. *go, sell what you own:* The call to renunciation of wealth is then clear and unambiguous, echoing both the teaching of Jesus (6:19–21,24–34) and the practice of the primitive Church (Acts 2:44). These allusions must be remembered in interpreting the meaning of Mt's addition of the phrase, "If you would be perfect." "Perfect" here does not designate a special state within the community of the disciples; the man does not become a disciple, and the only invitation Jesus gives him is the call to renounce his wealth. As in 5:48 (Mt's only two uses of the word), "perfect" designates the quality of discipleship. The man is not invited to practice "evangelical counsels," but, as in Mk, to become a disciple of Jesus. 22. The invitation is refused.

23. *it will be hard for a rich man:* The dialogue with the youth is followed by a saying of Jesus about riches and the reign; "reign" here suggests the idea of kingdom. Matthew omits the astonishment of the disciples and the repetition of the saying; this reflects the slowness of the disciples to understand, a trait that the Evangelist usually softens. 24. *easier for a camel:*

The figure of the camel and the eye of the needle means exactly what is said; it does not refer to a cable or a small gate of Jerusalem. 25. *who can be saved:* The response of the disciples shows that they understood the saying clearly enough. Their question shows no great perception of the principles enunciated in such passages as the eight beatitudes. In popular Jewish belief wealth was one of the rewards God conferred upon righteousness; and the saying of Jesus was more paradoxical than modern readers perceive. 26. The paradox is not softened by the saying that what is impossible with men is possible to God, and this does not mean that it is possible by a miracle for the rich to retain their wealth and still be saved. It means that God makes possible what man finds impossible—the renunciation of riches.

27. *then Peter said:* The question of Peter at this point seems to fall to a lower level; and Jesus' answer (Mk 10:29–30) makes no effort to raise the level. The reward of renunciation is put in terms that suit the tone of the question; and there may be more irony in the answer than most interpreters suspect. Matthew has tried to spiritualize the answer by compressing Mk's enumeration of the goods to be received a hundredfold and by the insertion of v. 28 (concerning the eschatological thrones). *judging the twelve tribes of Israel:* "Judge" is used here in the OT sense of "rule," not of passing a verdict. The Twelve are the leaders of the Church, and their position will be vindicated in the eschatological judgment. 29. *manyfold:* The ironical answer concerning the "manyfold" (Mk, "hundredfold") may be couched in terms that reflect the communism of goods of the primitive Church; all will enjoy common possessions equally. The saying then returns to the words "eternal life," with which the passage began, and the question of the man is finally and fully answered. But the final answer is not the answer Jesus gave in 19:17. The dialogue, as we have seen, is constructed in a pedagogical manner. The answer given in terms of Jewish morality leads step by step to the revolution of Christian morality; and only then is it stated clearly that Jewish morality, unless it leads to the fullness of the gospel, does not serve its purpose.

30. This statement, which cryptically alludes to the reversal of social positions in the reign, is also found in 20:16, where it is better suited to the context.

BOOK FIVE: JUDEA AND JERUSALEM (19:1–25:46)

(d) The Parable of the Laborers in the Vineyard (20:1–16)

This parable appears only in Mt; and it seems that it belongs to the "Jewish" Christians. No parable better illustrates the principle that allegorical interpretation is to be employed with great reserve; the vineyard, the denarius, the hours of the day when the men are hired, and the reverse order of payment have all been exploited for allegorical meaning. But the allegorical interpretations miss the point, and are mostly in contradiction with each other. The parable illustrates the dreadful condition of casual labor in the Hellenistic-Roman world, but that is not the point. 1. *to hire laborers:* Employers looked in the agora of the city for unemployed men waiting there to be hired. Such men worked for as little as the employer would pay. 2. *denarius:* A coin representing subsistence wages at the lowest level for a day. As the day goes on and more laborers are needed, more are hired at the same wage. 11. *they grumbled:* The dissatisfaction might seem reasonable to us; but the capitalist of the ancient world was master of his money, as the employer says (20:15). 14–15. The laborers are rebuked not for dissatisfaction with what they receive, but for dissatisfaction that others receive as much; and the employer insists on his right to be generous. By giving to one he takes nothing away from another.

The most obvious meaning of the parable is that it compares Jews and Gentiles in the reign; the Gentiles are admitted late, but they are admitted on an equal standing with the Jews. We know that the controversy over the admission of Gentiles was the major problem of the apostolic Church, and that it was ultimately resolved in the manner indicated in the parable. The parable must reflect this experience. 16. The saying does not really suit this situation because it is not a question of a reversal of positions—unless we suppose that from the Jewish-Christian point of view the admission of Gentiles on an equal plane was a degrading of the Jews.

But this parable, like others, may have several levels of meaning. Supposing that the interpretation indicated— the interpretation most widely accepted by the commentators—is the primary and basic interpretation, the position of the parable in the Gospel suggests that it may look in more than one direction. It is preceded by the promise that the Twelve will sit on 12 thrones, and it is followed very shortly by the request of the sons of Zebedee for the first places in the reign. Thus the parable may look not only to Jewish Christians as contrasted with Gentile Christians, but also at early disciples—even the Twelve— and others who became disciples much later. The parable indicates that an early call has no relevance to standing in the reign of God. Whenever one is admitted, one is admitted to full participation; the reign does not become the property of those who first sought admission, even if they are its officers.

(e) The Third Prediction of the Passion (20:17–19)

See the first two predictions: 16:21 and 17:22–23. The predictions are evidently arranged in such a way that they increase in vividness and detail. Mt alone mentions the crucifixion, but all three versions of the predictions reflect the passion narratives. Mt, following Mk (10:32–34), mentions the betrayal, the condemnation by the Jewish council, and the execution of the sentence by the Romans ("the Gentiles"). Mt omits the wonder and fear the disciples exhibit when Jesus begins to lead them to Jerusalem; the emphasis falls upon the fact that Jesus foretold the events of the future.

(f) The Sons of Zebedee (20:20–28)

Lk 22:24–27 contains only the second part of the saying (= Mt 20:24–28) in a different context and in a different form; and this saying very probably was found both in Mk (10:35–45) and in Q. The boldness of the request of the two disciples and the depth of misunderstanding it implies is sufficient explanation for Lk's omission of the request. Matthew has softened the request in his own way by introducing the mother as the petitioner; but she does not appear after 20:21. Though Matthew adds the mention of the mother, he abbreviates the request. The petition reflects popular messianic belief; but allusions to the glory of the Messiah are not missing in the Gospels, and it would be rather bold to say that Jesus never mentioned it. At the same time, the setting of the petition in the context immediately following the third prediction clearly emphasizes the common theme of the Gospels that the disciples did not grasp the reality of the sufferings of the Messiah. 21. *that my two sons may sit*: The petition asks for the two first places; and the petition is related to the question of precedence in 18:1–5. This does not imply that it is merely a doublet of the earlier question; no doubt more than one saying circulated about this highly important principle. 22. *are you able to drink the cup*: The answer of Jesus uses the metaphor of cup for suffering but omits Mk's metaphor of baptism, both used elsewhere. This association Jesus promises them. 23. *prepared by my Father*: By referring the assignment of places to the Father, Jesus says nothing about his personal relations

Book Five: Judea and Jerusalem (19:1—25:46)

to the Father but simply removes the question from discussion (see 24:36). The saying about the cup is certainly not couched in a form determined by later events. James was executed by Herod Agrippa in AD 42 (Acts 12:2); but the NT knows nothing of any tradition about a martyrdom of John.

24. *when the ten heard it*: The indignation of the disciples is easy to understand; but it arose from the same motives that prompted the petition of the two disciples and is therefore rebuked by Jesus. The position of the leaders in the Church is contrasted with the position of the rulers of the nations; the type of rule described suggests the courts of Hellenistic kings and of satellite kings in the Roman empire such as Herod. 25. *lord it over . . . exercise authority*: These words indicate absolute authority. This was the type of rule familiar to most subjects in the ancient world; Jesus is not judging this use of power favorably, nor is he condemning it. He simply describes existing institutions. 26. But absolute power is not to be used by the leaders in his Church. If the leaders wish to know how they should use their authority, they should consider that in the Church, social positions have been reversed; leaders in the Church are to be slaves. In the ancient world the slave was legally not a human person. This represents the lowest social stage (like the child in 18:2–4), the class of persons who are unable to impose their will on anyone but must suffer the imposition of the will of others. 27. This is the position that the first among the disciples should consider proper to himself in the Church. 28. Jesus adds that this is his own position. He has become the servant of all, and the service that is imposed upon him is the supreme sacrifice of life. It should be noticed that the term "ransom" follows the context of service. The ransom, the price paid, means that Jesus describes himself as reduced to the level of a means by which a purpose is achieved for others. The value of his life is determined not by self-assertion or self-aggrandizement even in a legitimate sense, but simply in terms of its value for other persons. This carries out the figure of the slave, who could have no personal ends to achieve.

(g) The Healing of Two Blind Men (20:29–34)

This is the final miracle story in the account of the public ministry of Jesus; it occurs just before the entrance into Jerusalem. Matthew has abbreviated Mk (10:46–52) by the omission of the name of the blind man and of picturesque details, but he has some interesting variations. As in the story of the demoniac of Gadara (8:28), he has two men instead of one. He adds the kind of detail that he usually omits and that is not given in Mk, the mention of Jesus' compassion and of his touching the eyes [→ Chapter 3: (A) Narrative Section: (l) Two Blind Men].

The story illustrates the rise of messianic feeling as Jesus approaches Jerusalem. Even blind men know who Jesus is, and they greet him with the Messianic title "Son of David" (see comment on 9:27). The impatience of the crowd with the noise of the beggars has no theological implications; it is simply a normal reaction to their importunity. When the blind men are cured, they follow Jesus—that is, they join the crowd that is gathering to accompany Jesus into Jerusalem. There is no longer any precept of silence nor any effort to restrain enthusiasm; Jesus is ready to enter Jerusalem acclaimed as Messiah because he will shortly demonstrate how the Messiah is to accomplish his saving act.

(h) The Entry into Jerusalem (21:1–9)

The action in this incident is continuous from the preceding passage; Mt, following Mk, puts all these episodes into a single day, the description of which ends at 21:17. The scene is a Messianic display. 1. *Bethphage*: The village, where the incident begins, cannot be precisely located; it lay on the slopes of the Mount of Olives. 2. *go into the village*: Matthew abbreviates the instructions of Jesus to the two disciples (see Mk 11:2–3). *a she-ass and a colt*: This is a striking variation from the colt mentioned in Mk; the alteration is made in view of 21:5. Matthew also omits Mk's account of how events proceeded according to the instructions of Jesus. 3. *the Lord*: It is not without interest that the Greek of 21:3 can also mean "The owner has need of them [it]." There is no other parallel in the Syn to the use of the title *Kyrios* in the sense in which it is used of Jesus in the Pauline epistles; this title was understood to belong to Jesus after his resurrection. 4. A fulfillment text is introduced (see comment on 1:22). The text is compiled from Is 62:11, the introductory line, and Zech 9:9, both quoted according to the LXX, but with the omission of a phrase in Zech that alludes to the victory of the king. The text of Zech includes the king among the "lowly" (see comment on 5:3,5) and lacks the usual traits of the royal messianic figure. Although only Mt quotes the verse, the scene appears to be a deliberate re-enactment of the prophetic saying. This was the only type of Messianic claim Jesus would publicly profess—the claim to be the Messiah who was one of the lowly. The mention of the ass and the colt in Zech is nothing but poetic parallelism,

Book Five: Judea and Jerusalem (19:1—25:46)

the use of two words to indicate a single animal; but Matthew has taken the verse with rigorous literalism; therefore he not only has the disciples take two animals but actually has Jesus riding both of them (21:7). The ride into Jerusalem then becomes a Messianic procession, with a large crowd taking part in the acclamations. 8. *spread their cloaks:* The spreading of cloaks in the paths was in imitation of the red-carpet treatment accorded royalty in the ancient world. *others cut branches:* The branches were also intended to soften the road. It is curious that none of the three Syn mentions the palms, which have become traditional in the liturgical commemoration of the procession; these occur in Jn 12:13. 9. *hosanna:* The acclamations of the crowd are based on Ps 118:25–26. The Hebr word *hôšî'āh-nā'* becomes in Gk *hōsanna* (really =Aram *hôša'-nā*), lit., "save, we pray"; but in these Gospel passages it has become a shout of acclamation with no regard to its meaning. *he who comes:* A Messianic title (see comment on 11:2); Mt adds "Son of David," a more explicit Messianic title (see comment on 9:2). The shout of *hōsanna* and the use of branches suggest the ritual of the Jewish Feast of Tabernacles.

(i) The Purging of the Temple (21:10–17)

Mk (11:15–19) places this episode on the day following Jesus' entry into Jerusalem, but Matthew makes it part of a climactic description of the first day of Jesus in Jerusalem. Mt alone relates that the whole city was stirred at his entry. 10. *stirred:* Lit., "shaken," the word that would be used to describe an earthquake. This effect on the whole city heightens the import of the Messianic procession. 11. *the prophet:* It is strange, however, that the Messianic titles do not appear in the words of "the crowds"; Jesus is not described as the king but as the prophet from Nazareth.

The purging of the Temple is put at the end of the public ministry by the Syn, at the beginning by Jn (2:13–22); Jn for his own reasons has adopted an artificial chronology. 12. *the Temple:* The Gk phrase *to hieron* designates the entire temple complex of courts and buildings. The business, however, could only have been transacted in the Court of the Gentiles, the outermost court into which any person could enter. The business was the sale of animals for sacrifice; the doves that were used by the poor as substitutes for the larger animals required of the wealthy are mentioned explicitly. *the money-changers:* Still a regular part of the Near Eastern urban scene, they performed a necessary service in a period when all sorts of coins were in circulation. It is assumed by commentators that these commercial services were a concession of the priests of the Temple; and it is difficult to see how such business could have been conducted without their participation. Jesus therefore attacked the Jerusalem hierocracy directly; this body appears rarely in the Gospels before the arrival in Jerusalem, but it is frequently mentioned thereafter. 13. *it is written*: Jesus justifies his action by a quotation of the OT combined from Is 56:7 and Jer 7:11 (quoted according to the LXX). Mt (and Lk) omit the phrase found in Mk (11:17), "for all nations." For Mt at least, the omission may be deliberate; the worship of the true God is to be communicated through Jesus the Messiah and not through the Temple of Jerusalem. The action of Jesus is a Messianic action. It corresponds to his assertion of supremacy over the Law (see 5:17–42; 12:1–14; 12:22–37). He asserts also his authority over the Temple, the second great institution of Judaism of the time. This leads to a question about his authority (see 21:23–27). By actions like this Jesus shows that he recognizes none of the existing authorities in Judaism; the implication that he has a greater authority is clear.

(j) The Cursing of the Fig Tree (21:18–19)

This episode is so difficult that it is omitted in Lk. Mt's abbreviations leave out some of the details, but the most startling alteration is that the fig tree withers instantly at the words of Jesus; in Mk the tree is seen to be withered when the party passes it on the following morning. Mk apparently has transformed a prophetic saying into a slow miracle, whereas Mt has transformed the slow miracle into an instantaneous miracle. The saying of Jesus is symbolic. It was not the season for the fig tree to bear fruit, but it did bear leaves. This is a symbol of Judaism, which has the appearance of religion without the reality. The words are addressed not to the fig tree but to Judaism; Judaism has come to its final crisis, and has rendered itself unproductive.

(k) The Interpretation of the Fig Tree (21:20–22)

The lesson of the fig tree is the same in Mt as in Mk, in spite of Mt's modifications in the cursing of the fig tree. But in neither Gospel can these sayings be in their original context. The withering of the fig tree becomes the occasion of sayings on faith, and the symbolism of the barren fig tree is

BOOK FIVE: JUDEA AND JERUSALEM (19:1—25:46)

left without explanation. Mt has already given these sayings in very nearly the same form (17:20); and Lk has them in a different context (17:6). Their attachment to the story of the fig tree is later than the transformation of the saying-story into a miracle story. This apparently had already happened in the sources of Mk.

(l) The Authority of Jesus (21:23-27)

Here Mt follows Mk (11:27-33) with no more than a few insignificant omissions. Both in Mt and Mk the question of the chief priests and elders (Mk adds "scribes") belongs properly after the purging of the Temple. Composition from various sources has put it back here, where it now refers to all of the words and works of Jesus. 23. *by what authority:* A question of a commission can refer only to his extraordinary act in purging the Temple. 24-25. The answer of Jesus is a counterquestion about the commission of John the Baptist. The Gospels reconstruct the attitude of the religious leaders of the Jews with little credit to the leaders; if they admit John's divine commission they convict themselves of unbelief, and if they deny it they risk inciting mob anger. Actually the evasion would have incited mob anger just as much; it is equivalently a refusal to recognize in John a man sent by God. The refusal of Jesus to answer the question about his own commission is a tacit rejection of the authority of the questioners. If they are religious leaders, teachers of the Law and cultic officers, they should be able to fulfill one of their fundamental responsibilities: to discern true and false prophets. 27. *we do not know:* They have professed themselves unable to reach a decision about the most prominent figure in their day before Jesus himself. This confession of incompetence releases Jesus from any obligation to submit himself to their judgment.

This is the first of five controversy stories in the days preceding the passion (see 22:15-22).

(m) The Parable of the Two Sons (21:28-32)

This parable, found only in Mt, stands as the first of three parables that deal with the same basic theme. The contrast between verbal rebellion and ultimate obedience as opposed to verbal obedience and failure to act is clear, and the adversaries themselves are compelled to admit that action is the test of obedience (see 7:21). 31. *tax collectors and prostitutes:* The application to the Jewish leaders contrasts them with the despised classes of tax collectors and prostitutes, who "push ahead" of them into the reign; the word is vivid. 32. *in a way of righteousness*: This does not mean that John led a righteous life but that he showed a way by which men could become righteous. The work the Jews profess but do not execute is not the observance of the Law but the work of faith. They have not admitted that the life of the Law leaves room for the repentance proclaimed by John and by Jesus as a condition of entrance into the reign. They have met the supreme demand of Judaism with professions of obedience. In its present form the parable no doubt reflects the faith of the Gentiles as contrasted with the unbelief of the Jews.

(n) The Parable of the Wicked Husbandmen (21:33–46)

Matthew has somewhat expanded this parable in order to make the point entirely clear, although the parable is not obscure in Mk. The description of the vineyard is given in words that closely echo Is 5:2, where the vineyard symbolizes Israel. The parable of Jesus has allegorical features. The owner is an absentee landlord, and in the NT world such disputes between landlords and tenants were not unknown. 34. *he sent his slaves*: Matthew increases the number of the slaves so that their allegorical significance may be completely clear; the slaves represent the prophets (see 23:29–31). 37. *he sent his son*: The allegorical significance of the son is not equally clear. No OT figure can be intended; and the death of John the Baptist cannot be attributed to the Jews. If the son is an allegorical figure, he can represent no one but Jesus; and one would expect more to be made of this feature of the parable. 38. *let us kill him*: As a suggestion that Jesus himself is the son who is killed, this passage is extremely delicate; that it is an ecclesiastical expansion inserted in the primitive Church seems unlikely, because it is a part of the climactic structure of the parable. Some scholars have proposed that the entire parable is of ecclesiastical origin; but most recent commentators do not favor this opinion, in spite of the allegorical elements in the parable.

The plan of the tenants to kill the son is not unrealistic, as J. Jeremias has pointed out (*The Parables of Jesus* [rev. ed.; N.Y., 1963] 76). When a proselyte died intestate, his property became unoccupied land that went to the first claimant; and the tenants had the first opportunity to claim by occupation. 41. It is not without interest that Mt, for which an Aram original is alleged, is the only one of the three Gospels that has a pure Gk play on words: "Evilly those evil men he will destroy." Mt heightens the tension by

Book Five: Judea and Jerusalem (19:1—25:46)

the dialogue form, which elicits the words of condemnation from the Jews themselves. The application of the parable is much more explicit in Mt than it is in Mk or Lk. 42. The quotation of Ps 118:22–23 (LXX) is applied in a broad sense; and as it stands it can refer only to the admission of the Gentiles to the Church. Quite possibly this biblical explanation of the parable is an ecclesiastical expansion. 43. The same is almost certainly to be said of Mt's addition, where the displacement of the Jews in favor of the Gentiles is suggested beyond all doubt. It was hardly necessary for Matthew to retain Mk's notice that the chief priests and Pharisees recognized that Jesus spoke about them. The high popular esteem in which Jesus was held kept them from action at the moment. This esteem is often attested in the Gospels; how deep it was cannot be said, but it should be remembered when the question of the general popular Jewish attitude toward Jesus arises. The agents of hostility in the passion narratives are the religious leaders of Judaism, not the mass of the people.

(o) The Parable of the Wedding Feast (22:1–14)

The dissimilarities in detail between Mt and Lk are so great that there is room for doubt that both Gospels are using the same source (Q); but the evidences of extensive rewriting in Mt are clear. Instead of a dinner Mt has a royal wedding feast; in addition to the excuses presented by the guests in Lk, Mt introduces a violently discordant note in the killing of the messengers and the ensuing war. This feature very probably represents the destruction of Jerusalem by the Romans in AD 70; it is not intruded into an existing form of the parable but is the reason for the change of the main figure of the parable from a host to a king. 8. *those invited were not worthy*: These guests are intended to signify both the Jewish people and their leaders; in Lk only the Jewish people as a whole are meant. In Lk the parable then proceeds to the call of the Gentiles, signified by the invitation of anyone who happens to be in the neighborhood. 11. Matthew has altered this part of the parable in such a way that it becomes a second parable. The theme of this modification is set by the introduction of the phrase "good and bad" (22:10). Even after the rejection of the guests first invited, one still appears who is not suitably attired for a wedding feast; a clean white garment was the proper dress for such festivities. This feature should not be forced into an allegorical significance. The point of the second parable is that the reign contains wicked as well as righteous, the same point that is made in the parables of the tares and the net (see 13:36–43,47–50). In these parables the mixed condition of the Church endures until the Judgment. **13**. Matthew by the use of his tag line (see 8:12; 13:42,50) introduces an eschatological note that changes the image of the wedding feast from the Church to the eschatological Messianic banquet. The punishment is instant and severe.

14. Language is used here that later became the language of predestination. No complex theological theory lies behind the verse. The parable represents God as making every effort to bring guests to the eschatological feast; the invitation to all who pass on the highways and byways, even "the good and the bad" (as contrasted with Lk's beggars, destitute, blind, and lame) is clear. All these are called; the chosen are those who accept the call and do not reject the invitation, like the first guests, or who do not accept it fully, like the man who comes to dinner but is too much of a boor to dress in the proper manner. Because the parable does not exhibit Matthew's usually fine literary unity and coherence, there is no reason to postulate a compilation from various sources; rather it is a rare example of substantial rewriting by Matthew; and it shows that he did not rewrite skillfully.

(p) The Question of Tribute Paid to Caesar (22:15–22)

This is the second of the five controversy-stories in this section (see 21:23–27). The narrative is taken from Mk (12:13–17) with only slight revisions; Lk (20:20–26) has altered it more extensively. **16.** *the Herodians:* The Pharisees make common cause with the Herodians to "trap" Jesus. The Herodians (see Mk 3:6) were supporters of the dynasty of Herod, represented at the time by Herod Antipas, tetrarch of Galilee. The Herodian fortunes were founded on unswerving loyalty to Rome; Herod the Great had proved this by magnificent political dexterity during the civil wars that followed the assassination of Julius Caesar. **17.** *taxes:* The position of the Herodians on the payment of the poll tax (Gk *kēnsos* =Lat *census*) exacted by the Romans was clear. The party of the Zealots refused to admit the subjection of the people of God to a foreign power; the theoretical position of the Pharisees was identical with the position of the Zealots, but they did not believe in the use of force to achieve independence. The question was bound to alienate one party or the other. The flattering words in which Jesus is addressed suggest that he was expected to take the Zealot position; this, as Lk (20:20) says, would render him liable to arrest. **18.** *Jesus perceived their malice:* In Mk mention is made of the "hypocrisy" of the Pharisees. **19.** *the tax coin:*

Book Five: Judea and Jerusalem (19:1—25:46)

Jesus calls for the actual coin, the denarius, for his answer. The right to mint coinage is an act of sovereignty, and it was jealously guarded by the Roman government. Satellite kings and free cities were permitted to issue coins, but it was clearly understood that this was done with Roman authorization. The minting of coins without authorization was an act of rebellion. 20. *whose likeness . . . :* The coin provides an answer to the question; it belongs to Caesar, and it is within his power to demand it.

Jesus thus rejects the position of the Zealots without accepting the position of the Herodians. Effectively his answer evades the question rather than solves it. He does not appeal to right but simply to the *de facto* existence of Caesar's power, symbolized by Caesar's coinage. Whether Caesar has a right to rule is not touched by the answer. The explanation, "Give Caesar what is his and God what is his," offers no basis for a theory of politics. Jesus certainly did not intend to divide the world into areas belonging to Caesar and God, each with his respective and exclusive jurisdiction. Nor did he answer the question what belongs to Caesar and what belongs to God. This he left to the personal decision of each man, who must solve the problem of the opposing claims of God and Caesar. The saying is valid here that no man can serve two masters (6:24).

(q) Marriage and the Resurrection (22:23-33)

This is the third of the controversy-stories in this series. The Sadducees are less well known in biblical and extrabiblical sources than the Pharisees. They were the party of the priestly aristocracy and seem to have represented the wealthy landowning class as well. They were thoroughly conservative. In politics they accepted the Roman rule of Palestine, and in theology they accepted only the Law as the basis of Judaism. They based their denial of the resurrection on the absence of the resurrection in the text of the Law.

Matthew has compressed Mk's account (12:18–27) without any significant change of the sense. The case presented to Jesus is intended by the Sadducees to show the absurdity of belief in the resurrection. 24. *if a man dies without children:* The very free citation of the law of the levirate is based on Dt 25:5–6 and Gn 38:8, but it is not an exact quotation of either text; and Matthew has abbreviated the citation. The law of the levirate provided for continuity of the family. When a man died without children, his brother was obliged to have a child by the widow; the child would bear the name of the deceased. 29. *you are wrong:* Jesus answers the case by denying the presupposition that marriage endures in the afterlife. The conception here is related to that expressed by Paul in 1 Cor 15:35–50; the resurrection is affirmed, but a transformation of the body is also affirmed. "Flesh and blood will not possess the reign." 30. *like angels in heaven:* The example of the angels refers to a life in which sex plays no part; it does not designate the absence of the bodily component in the afterlife, for this would itself be a denial of the resurrection and an affirmation of Platonic immortality.

31–32. These verses are a supplementary argument about the resurrection independent of the question about the seven brothers. The Sadducees denied the resurrection because they could not find it in the Law. 32. The argument of Jesus, genuinely rabbinical in character, is based on Ex 3:6. The patriarchs had been long dead when God spoke to Moses, yet God *is* the God of Abraham, Isaac, and Jacob. This he could not be if they had ceased to exist; therefore they must live in some way other than the life of the terrestrial body. The answer does indeed raise questions, but the Sadducees were unable to answer them. In their doctrine there was no relation between God and the dead, and they could not explain this text.

(r) The Greatest Commandment (22:34–40)

This is the fourth of the controversy-stories. The three Syn diverge more than usual in their versions of this incident. Lk (10:25–28) has placed it in a different context and has appended to the discussion the parable of the Good Samaritan, peculiar to itself; the classic exposition of the meaning of the term "neighbor." Lk also makes the "lawyer" (more frequently "scribe," and always "scribe" in Mt except here) state the two commandments in answer to the question of Jesus. Mk, particularly by the addition of 12:32–34 (peculiar to itself), presents the scribe in a favorable light, and Jesus praises his answer. In Mt and Lk, however, the questioner is hostile and asks the question to "tempt" Jesus; in Mt he speaks as the representative of a conspiracy. Mt regularly views the scribes and Pharisees in a less friendly manner than the other Gospels.

36. *which is the greatest commandment:* The question is placed in terms of the rabbinical understanding of the Law. The rabbis counted 613 distinct commandments in the Law, of which 248 were positive precepts and 365 were prohibitions. These commandments were distinguished as "light" and "heavy" according to the seriousness of the subject. This type of question was normal in rabbinical discussion, and it is difficult to see how

it could have been conceived as a "trial" of Jesus. On the other hand, he is represented as claiming the power to interpret the Law independently and even to restate it. **37.** *you shall love . . .* : The answer of Jesus quotes two texts of the Law that form the foundation of the new morality of the gospel. The commandments are quoted from Dt 6:5 and Lv 19:18. The text of Dt 6:5 forms a part of the Shema, the Jewish profession of faith; Mk quotes 6:4, the introductory verse. The novelty of the statement of Jesus does not consist in quoting this commandment; no rabbi could have called this anything but an excellent answer. The novelty consists in placing Lv 19:18 on the same level, making it equally "heavy." To this arrangement of the two commandments so that they become effectively one there is no parallel in Jewish literature. The *T. Issachar* (5:2 [*APOT* 2, 327]), often quoted in this connection, does indeed urge the love of God and of the neighbor; but these are not stated as the two greatest commandments of the Law, nor are they so explicitly given equal weight. **40.** *on these two commandments:* Mt alone adds that on these commandments "hang" the Law and the Prophets—that is, the entire revelation of the OT. Good works have value as acts of the love of God and of the neighbor.

(s) The Son of David (22:41–46)

This is the fifth and last of the controversy-stories. Up to this point Jesus has responded to questions; now he himself puts an exegetical question to the Pharisees, which they cannot answer. Mt makes it much more explicit that he "tests" the Pharisees; in Mk (12:35–37a) he "teaches," and in Lk (20:41–44) he continues his discourse. **42.** *whose son is he:* In Mt the affirmation that the Messiah is the son (descendant) of David is elicited from the Pharisees. The Gk and the Eng versions of Ps 110:1 (quoted from the LXX except for one word) contain an ambiguity not found in the MT. The Jews of this period did not pronounce the divine name Yahweh, but substituted for it the title *'ădōnāy*, "lord" (lit., "my lords," a grammatical form used only of the deity); *'ădōnî* "my lord," is in the OT the usual form of address to a king. Thus the Greek represents the pronunciation of the verse used at the time: " *'ădōnāy* said to *'ădōnî*," instead of "*Yahweh* said to *'ădōnî*." The question assumes several accepted rabbinical views in terms of which the question is put and within which it would have to be answered: (1) David wrote "in the spirit," under divine inspiration; (2) David is the author of Ps 110; (3) *'ădōnî* designates the Messiah. The modern exegete would solve the problem by rejecting the authorship of David and the assumptions of (3). Within Jewish exegetical tradition this could not be done, and the problem remained insoluble. 45. The saying is obscure, and modern commentators differ in its interpretation. That Jesus meant to "teach" anything by proposing a question his adversaries could not solve and he did not solve seems doubtful. The question implies no claim of his own to the title of Messiah and Son of David; such a claim would have to be discussed on the basis of other texts. Nor does the question imply a rejection of the idea of king Messiah and Son of David. Jesus certainly did reject most aspects of the popular understanding of the king Messiah, but he does not do it here. Nor does he imply a deeper and mysterious reality in virtue of which the Messiah is both son of David and David's lord; this again would have to be discussed on the basis of other texts. The point of the story is that the Pharisees could not solve a simple exegetical problem. Jesus thus demonstrates that they are not competent religious teachers; even their vaunted skill of interpretation breaks down. They cannot be judges of the identity of the Messiah if they cannot deal with a messianic text. Whether they accept Jesus as the Messiah or not is meaningless because they do not understand the Scriptures in which the Messiah is revealed.

(t) Invective Against the Scribes and Pharisees (23:1–36)

Chapter 23 is a construction of Mt like the discourses previously noticed. In its present position it serves both as a conclusion of the controversy-stories and as an introduction to the eschatological discourse that follows (see 23:36). Mk has a much briefer invective against the Pharisees, but Matthew has made little use of Mk (12:37b-40). Some of the sayings come from Q (Lk 20:45–47; 11:39–51 par.), and the rest of the chapter is peculiar to Mt. The discourse frequently reflects the controversies between Jews and Jewish Christians; in its present form it clearly conveys the experiences of the Palestinian church and the fall of Jerusalem in AD 70. The discourse is composed of an introduction, seven woes against the scribes and Pharisees, and a conclusion. Mk speaks only of the scribes; Lk divides the woes between the scribes and the Pharisees. In all three Gospels the discourse is delivered to a crowd; Mt and Lk mention the disciples explicitly.

Book Five: Judea and Jerusalem (19:1—25:46)

(i) Introduction (23:1-12)

1. *the chair of Moses:* This designation of a teacher's podium is otherwise attested for the 4th cent. AD but not for NT times. The phrase is most probably a metaphor for the authority of the scribes to teach. In rabbinical tradition the interpretation of the Law was carried on in a scribal tradition that theoretically went back through an unbroken chain of scribes to Moses. This view is, of course, entirely unhistorical. Jesus does not discuss the historical character of the tradition, nor does he question the authority of the scribes to teach. The basis of this authority was no more than custom in the post-exilic Jewish community; the scribes grew up with the development of the Law as the basis of Jewish religion and life. **3.** *observe and do what they tell you:* Jesus does not attack the teaching of the scribes; actually there is a lack of consistency between this general statement and some particular interpretations of the Law that are discussed in Mt (see 5:17-42; 12:1-14; 15:1-20; 19:1-12). The position of Jesus toward the Law was variously interpreted in the apostolic Church (see 5:17-20), and for this reason the position of the apostolic Church was not clear and firm from the beginning. It can be said, however, that the Gospels contain no formal and total repudiation of the teaching authority of the scribes. What is principally criticized here is not the teaching of the scribes but their practice; it does not cohere with their teaching. **4-6.** These verses state two complaints: the rigor of scribal interpretation and the vanity and hypocrisy of the scribes and Pharisees (see 6:1-8,16-18). A general statement that scribal teaching is always rigorous would go too far. The text deals with attitudes, not with particulars, and the influence of Pharisaic theory and practice on interpretation led to a severe rather than a humane interpretation of the Law. This is verified not only by the incidents recorded in the Gospels but also by the Talmud. Rabbis themselves were sometimes as critical of rigorism as are the Gospels. The second complaint—vanity and hypocrisy—is expanded in 23:5-6, and it runs through much of the discourse. Jesus echoes the ancient prophetic charge of mere formalism in religion and adds to it the charge of vain display. **5.** *phylacteries:* Small boxes containing parchment on which is written the text of Ex 13:1-16; Dt 6:4-9 and 11:13-21. These were fastened to the left wrist and to the forehead in such a way that they hung in front of the eyes. Thus the injunction to keep the Law as a sign on the hand and as a memorial between the eyes (Ex 13:9; Dt 6:8; 11:18) was literally observed. *tassels:* On the four corners of the cloak tassels were worn in observance of Nm 15:38-39 as reminders of the Law. The size of these was obviously a token of great devotion; one need not look far for parallels in Christian devotional practices. 6. *the place of honor at feasts:* The desire for such places in synagogues or at dinners is not well supported by the Talmud. These are ordinary marks of human vanity, and the protocol of precedence in modern times is as rigorous as anything found in Pharisaism. 7. *salutations:* Near Eastern courtesy demanded that the length of the salutation be in proportion to the dignity of the person, and thus the greeting was a status symbol. This should be remembered. *rabbi:* The Aram title, "my master," was used for a teacher of the Law; it is attested for NT times only in the NT; but it appears in postbiblical Judaism and must have been coming into use at this time. The term or the Gk equivalent is often used by those who address Jesus in the Gospels.

8–12. These verses echo the theme of 18:1–5 and 20:23–28 and appear to be a digression originally unconnected with the invective against the scribes and Pharisees. Three honorific scribal titles are rejected: master (Aram *rabbî*), father (Aram *'abbā*), and teacher (Hebr *môrēh*). The title of "father" is not well attested in Jewish literature, but the text does not indicate that it was common. 8. Honorific titles are rejected because the disciples are all brothers—there is one Father, God; and one teacher, the Messiah. Scarcely any verse in the Gospels is so clearly an ecclesiastical expansion as this one. This text would seem to exclude all honorific titles within the community of the disciples; Christian tradition has taken this verse in an extremely restricted literal sense, and even in this restricted interpretation has found room for the modern clerical title of "Father." Other honorific titles have not been considered excluded by this verse. 11. A repetition of 20:26. 12. This verse is used twice by Lk in different contexts (14:11; 18:14). The sense is not that one should await the place that God finally grants.

(ii) The first woe (23:13)

The metaphor of the keys of the reign, used of Peter in 16:19, is applied to the scribes and Pharisees. The reign here means the reign inaugurated by the proclamation of Jesus. The Pharisees refuse to believe in Jesus, and they exclude from the Jewish community those who do believe. This modification of Lk 11:52 again seems to be an ecclesiastical expansion; Lk has a more difficult phrase, "the key of knowledge," which seems to be more original. 14. This verse (Mk 12:40 par.) does not belong to the critical text of Mt and is omitted by modern editors.

BOOK FIVE: JUDEA AND JERUSALEM (19:1—25:46)

(iii) The second woe (23:15)

There is ample evidence that Jewish proselytism was extremely active in NT times. This missionary activity came to an end with the Jewish War and the destruction of Jerusalem in AD 70. *proselyte:* As contrasted with "the fearer of God," he accepted circumcision and the full observance of the Law. The "fearers of God" professed faith in one God and attended the synagogue but did not become full members of the Jewish community. *twice as much a son of Gehenna:* This is a very forceful expletive, and it is difficult to discern what lay at the base of this severe condemnation of proselytes. The verse must, it seems, reflect the experience of the apostolic Church (and most probably, as elsewhere in this discourse, the Jewish Christian community). It is very possible that proselytes showed greater hostility toward Jewish Christians, whom they regarded as renegades, than native Jews did.

(iv) The third woe (23:16-22)

Here Pharisaic teaching is criticized. On the problem of oaths see 5:33-37. 16. *blind guides:* See 15:14. The point at issue is the rabbinical teaching on the obligation of oaths. The examples used cannot be paralleled from the Talmud, but the principle that is attacked is easy to identify. The question is whether or not the formula of an oath is to be regarded as obligatory. One who wished to evade the obligation could seek out an interpretation that denied the validity of the formula used. One might illustrate in modern terms by saying that an oath by God would oblige, but an oath by Gosh or by Golly would not. The casuistry of such evasions is what Jesus attacks. If a man intends to swear, he swears. If he intends that another should think he swears, but deliberately uses a formula that he believes is invalid, he swears. This passage, like 5:33-37, is peculiar to Mt; and in these discussions of rabbinical casuistry we have the traditions of the Palestinian Christian community. But the vigor with which these evasions of truthfulness are attacked goes back to the source of the Gospel.

(v) The fourth woe (23:23-24)

This woe again attacks the teaching of the scribes and Pharisees. The question at issue was what forms of produce came under the law of tithing. In the rigorist interpretation every natural growth was subject to the law; a more humane interpretation would limit the obligation to the traditional "grain, wine, and oil." Mint, dill, and cumin are examples of tiny seeds or plants, which it would be ridiculous to tithe. But Jesus does not object to this rigor in itself; he objects to the interest shown in such trivia while the "heavy" commandments (see 22:34–40) are ignored. The heavy commandments are cited as "judgment" (equivalent to "justice"), mercy, and fidelity. An example of the difficulty Gentile Christians had in apprehending such a thoroughly Jewish passage as this can be seen in Lk 11:42, which is put in much more general terms. 24. *you strain at a gnat:* The final touch of ridicule is the example of straining out the gnat and swallowing the camel. In the ancient world, strainers were commonly attached to the mouths of decanters because any liquid might contain foreign matter. Pharisaic observance used the strainer not only for this purpose but also to strain out any unclean substance that one might inadvertently consume. Casuistry can get so lost in details that it forgets to ask simple questions like Is this fair? Is it decent? The camel was the largest animal known to Palestinians; to judge by the use of the camel in figures like this and in 19:24, such hyperbole was common in popular speech.

(vi) *The fifth woe (23:25–26)*

In some instances Pharisaic devotion to cleanliness approached the fanatic (see 15:1–20). The dish and the cup here are not, however, meant literally; it is doubtful that Pharisaic practice would be content with washing the outside of the vessel. The vessels are metaphors for the person; and the woe is directed at the care for external correctness in observance without regard for the interior disposition. The vices mentioned are "plunder," not otherwise mentioned in Mt (but see Mk 12:40), and "intemperance," which is so remotely associated with plunder that the mss. have several variations, of which the colorless "injustice" is the favorite. The combination, however, does echo Am 2:6–8.

(vii) *The sixth woe (23:27–28)*

These lines are similar in structure to the preceding woe. The whitewashing of tombs in present-day Palestine dates back to NT times, when it was common practice. Since contact with death caused Levitical uncleanness, the whitewashing served to identify the tombs and ward off those who

Book Five: Judea and Jerusalem (19:1—25:46)

might otherwise touch them accidentally. The interior of the tomb was the supreme degree of uncleanness and the figure is strong. 28. The point is again Pharisaic practice. The vices cited are hypocrisy (the word is a refrain in the discourse) and lawlessness; the observance of the Law, of which the Pharisees boasted, was a cloak for a life that was lived in complete contradiction with the Law.

(viii) The seventh woe (23:29-36)

This is the longest of the seven, and it no doubt reflects the execution of Jesus, the Messiah and the ultimate fulfillment of prophecy, and the attacks of Jewish authorities against the apostles and missionaries of the primitive Christian community. Hostility to the prophets is traced back in an unbroken chain to the origins of the nation—indeed, to the origins of humanity, for the series begins with Abel; and Israel could hardly be blamed for his death. The hostility of Israel to the prophets is somewhat schematized, just as Ezekiel traces the rebellion of Israel to its origins (Ez 16). There are few instances in the OT of prophets who were killed by the Israelites, nor is the number notably increased in the folklore of the apocryphal literature. The argument by which the present generation of Jews is linked with its ancestors in the killing of the prophets is somewhat involved and rabbinical in character.

29. *you build the tombs of the prophets:* By building the tombs of the prophets and disclaiming the actions of the ancestors, the Jews confess that they are sons of prophet-killers; and by the peculiar Hebr conception of sonship the designation, which they themselves accept, shows that they have the dispositions of their fathers. 32. *fill up the measure of your fathers:* That is, by continuing to kill prophets. 33. *brood of vipers:* See 3:7; 12:34. *being condemned to Gehenna:* The fate is inevitable. The whole passage is to be read in the light of the catastrophe of AD 70, but condemnation to Gehenna goes beyond God's judgments in history. 34. *I will send you prophets:* The sending of "prophets, wise men, and scribes" (Lk 11:49, "prophets and apostles," a more candid allusion to Christian missionaries) is conceived in the same terms we find in Is 6:9-10 (see 13:10-15) and Ex 4:21; 7:3; 10:20,27. The benevolent purpose of divine revelation is frustrated by the unbelief of men, and the effect of the revelation is to harden the hearts of those who refuse to receive it. 35. *from the blood of Abel:* The collective guilt of the murder of all the innocent from Abel to Zechariah is indeed a terrible

load to bear; and it is here especially that the passage is to be understood in the light of the great catastrophe of AD 70, in which Jerusalem and the Temple were destroyed and thousands of Jews perished. To those who were accustomed to think biblically this event was a manifest judgment of God; and the horror of the disaster showed that it was a judgment for no ordinary crime but suitable to a vast burden of guilt. Abel (Gn 4:8) is the first victim of murder in the Bible; and the prophet Zechariah (2 Chr 24:20–22), killed in the reign of Joash of Judah, is the last victim of murder in the Hebr Bible, in which the books of Chronicles stand last. This is no doubt the reason why these two names are mentioned. "Zechariah" has been an exegetical problem: In 2 Chr 24:20 he is called the son of Jehoiada. The only Zechariah the son of Berechiah is the eleventh of the twelve prophets (Zech 1:1); but some uncertainty about his patronymic is excusable inasmuch as he is called the son of Iddo in Ezr 5:1, his grandfather in Zech 1:1. There is no doubt a confusion of the patronymics in the tradition; Zechariah the minor prophet was a much better known figure than the Zechariah of 2 Chr 24. The difficulty, however, has led some interpreters to identify Zechariah with Zechariah the son of Baris, killed in AD 70 shortly before the fall of the Temple (Josephus, JW 4.5,4 § 335). All this blood comes upon this generation in the war with the Romans.

(ix) Conclusion (23:37–39)

The apostrophe to Jerusalem, taken from Q, is placed in Lk (13:34–35) in a different context at the departure of Jesus from Galilee. In both Gospels a different phrase appears, which permits the verses to follow easily from what precedes, and there is no reason to think that either Gospel represents the original context or that the saying was preserved with any context. 37. *killing and stoning:* The allusion again seems to reflect the experience of the early Christian missionaries. 38. *your house will be left you:* The prediction echoes such prophetic passages as Jer 12:7; 22:5; Ez 10:18–19; 11:22–23, in which Yahweh is said to depart from Jerusalem. 39. In Lk the final verse could refer to the entrance of Jesus into Jerusalem (see 20:9 par. Lk 19:38); but by placing the prediction here, Matthew has made the eschatological reference clear beyond doubt. The coming to which Jerusalem can look is the parousia of the Son of Man; and thus the discourse leads into the great eschatological discourse that follows. It is probably because of this close

Book Five: Judea and Jerusalem (19:1—25:46)

connection that Mt omits the story of the widow's mite (Mk 12:41–44 par. Lk 21:1–4).

(B) Discourse: The Eschatological Sermon (24:1—25:46)

The basis of Mt 24 is Mk 13. The eschatological discourse is the only portion of Mk that can properly be called a discourse; this was plainly the most important collection of the sayings of Jesus in the circles in which the Gospel of Mk arose. Matthew has expanded the discourse in ch. 25 by the use of materials from Q and from private sources.

The ambiguous attitude of the apostolic Church toward the parousia of the Son of Man and the end of the world is a celebrated exegetical and theological question that cannot be settled here. But the materials of Mt's discourse must be employed in reaching an understanding of the attitude of the apostolic Church, and they should be explained clearly and objectively. The discourse refers both to the fall of Jerusalem and to the eschatological end; but it is impossible to sort out which verses refer to which event. One must understand that in much biblical thinking, both in the OT and in the NT, history and eschatology are merged in a way that is alien to modern thought. Particular historical events that are seen as judgments of God are described in eschatological terms; the examples are too numerous for citation here, but one may mention the fall of Jerusalem in 587 BC, the fall of the Assyrian and the Babylonian kingdoms, and even minor historical events such as the fall of Edom and the fall of Tyre. A blurring of perspective in the consideration of the fall of Jerusalem, far from being strange to the thought and language of Judaism, is native to it. Jesus did not depart from biblical language; and the precedents for such language in the prophetic literature were numerous enough to preclude that type of misunderstanding that would identify the fall of Jerusalem with the beginning of the end catastrophe.

This sermon must also be read with the awareness that its composition was affected by the fact that the catastrophe of Jerusalem had already occurred; the narratives describe an event that was remembered. This is not to say that Jesus did not predict it; but his exact words were not remembered any more precisely for this than for other sayings, and the historical impact of the event could hardly have been conducive to a more accurate preservation of them.

It is the reality of the eschatological event that is the object of the discourse, not its date. There are clear warnings—not necessarily original—against attempting to calculate the date. The point is that man in history lives under an eschatological judgment, which means a final judgment. In particular events, such as the fall of Jerusalem, the judgment seems to break into history. When it does, it reminds man of his eschatological destiny; and he is warned in terms such as those used in Mt 25 that the judgment is to be awaited with unremitting vigilance. There is a sense in which the eschatological judgment can and must always be conceived as "near"; for there is no one to whom it is irrelevant.

(a) The Prediction of the Destruction of the Temple (24:1–3)

In 21:23 Mt has presented Jesus entering the Temple; in the chapters that follow controversies and invective against the Pharisees occupy the period since that entry. Here in 24:1 Mt depicts Jesus leaving the Temple and arriving at the Mt. of Olives (24:3). The change of locale is rather sudden; the rough transition is due to a compilation in Mk (13:1–4), which in Mt is somewhat smoothed over.

The remarks of the disciples allude to the restoration of the Second Temple initiated by Herod the Great in 19 BC (Josephus, *JW* 1.21, 1 § 401; but cf. *Ant.* 15.11, 1 § 380). The reconstruction was finished by the time of Jesus' public ministry; the 46 years of Jn 2:20 would place the period in AD 26–27. But embellishment of the structure was continued until AD 66; all work was completed only four years before the Temple was destroyed by fire in AD 70. The observations about the size of the stones in Mk are fully justified by the remains of Herodian masonry in Palestine. Jesus' comment on the remarks of the disciples includes a prediction that introduces a somber note.

The western slope of the Mt. of Olives affords the best panorama of the city of Jerusalem. In NT times the Temple occupied the prominent position in the foreground, roughly where the Dome of the Rock now stands.

Matthew has made two changes in Mk (13:1–4): The discourse is addressed to all the disciples instead of to Peter, Andrew, James, and John; and the question of the disciples is made more clearly eschatological. 3. The disciples in Mk and Lk ask vaguely when "these things" will happen; in the context the question refers to the prediction of the destruction of the temple. Mt adds to this the question of the sign of the parousia of Jesus and

BOOK FIVE: JUDEA AND JERUSALEM (19:1—25:46)

the end of the world. Both these phrases are used only by Mt in the Gospels, and parousia is used only in Mt 24–25. The word *parousia* in Hellenistic Greek designated either the manifestation of a hidden god or the visit of an emperor or potentate to a city. In the NT and later Christian literature it becomes a technical term for the Second Coming of Jesus. The question is framed by Mt from the contents of the discourse.

(b) The Signs of the Parousia (24:4–8)

The sermon proper begins with a warning against deception. 4. *many will come*: This claim to be the Messiah is generally ascribed to a number of Jewish rebels against Rome before the outbreak of the Jewish War. Mt introduces the word "Messiah" into the claim (cf. Mk 13:5). 6. Widespread wars, earthquakes, and famine are commonplaces in biblical and extrabiblical apocalyptic literature. There can be no allusion to events contemporary with the composition of the Gospel unless we suppose that the author exaggerates the Jewish War into a cosmic catastrophe, which he may very well do according to the principle mentioned [→ Chapter 6: (B) Discourse]. 8. *the beginning*: But the disciples are not to take these events as "the end"; they are the beginning of the birth pangs. "The birth pangs of the Messiah" are a designation of convulsions in nature and in history that usher in the Messianic era; the term is used in rabbinical literature.

(c) Persecutions and Dissensions (24:9–14)

Mt deviates from Mk in this section because Matthew has already used Mk's material in the missionary discourse (10:17–21); 24:9b parallels Mk 13:13a, and 24:13 (Mk 13:13b par.) is repeated from 10:22b. The material peculiar to Mt does not refer to persecutions but to dissensions within the Church; scandal, mutual distrust and hatred, betrayal, and deception through false prophets (see 13:36–43,47–50). This is summed up as the growth of lawlessness to the point where love grows cold. Here again no allusion to events contemporary with the writing of the Gospel can be traced; but little is known of the conditions of the Jewish-Christian community in Palestine during the years of the Jewish War. Mt 24:14 parallels Mk 13:10; this line, by virtue of its transfer to this position, leads clearly into the following section and strengthens the eschatological thrust of Mt's form of the discourse. The proclamation of the Gospel to all nations is a gradual development in the Gospels; but only here is the fulfillment of the mission made a sign of the near approach of the end. Thus Mt's reconstruction suggests that what follows is to be referred to the end; this suggestion is not made in the versions of Mk and Lk.

(d) The Abomination of Desolation (24:15–22)

In spite of the last verse of the preceding section, these lines are quite clearly referred to the Jewish War. **15.** *the abomination of desolation:* Cf. Dn 9:27; 12:11 [LXX]. In Dn the abomination signifies the erection of the image of Zeus Olympios in the Jerusalem Temple by Antiochus IV Epiphanes in 168 BC. Luke (21:20–24) is quite correct in referring this sign here explicitly to the presence of hostile forces; he omits the Hebr phrase as scarcely intelligible to Gentile readers—or to himself. *let the reader* [of Dn] *understand:* An occult interpretation of Dn is intended. This is a warning to the Palestinian Christian community to escape. A tradition preserved by Eusebius (*HE* 3.5,3) relates that the Palestinian Christians fled to Pella in the northern valley of the Jordan to escape the Jewish War. **16.** Oddly enough this town is not in "the mountains," i.e., the hills of the desert of Judea. The escape must be made with no delay. **17.** *he who is on the roof:* The roof of Palestinian houses was reached by an outside stairway; one who must flee should leave at once without trying to bring anything from the house. **18.** The man who is plowing should not even go back to the edge of the field where he left his cloak. **19.** The note of compassion for pregnant women and nursing mothers is obvious; so is flight in the rainy season, when one is exposed to rain and chilly weather. **20.** *on a Sabbath:* But the allusion to flight on the Sabbath is meaningful only to Jewish Christians who observe the Sabbath, a day on which a journey in excess of 2000 paces was prohibited in rabbinical interpretation. **21.** *such as have not been:* The troubles of the Jewish War are described by hyperbole in a phrase based on Dn 12:1 as the greatest in human history. The "salvation," which no one would attain unless the time of tribulation were shortened, does not mean spiritual salvation but escape from death; unless God mercifully shortened the time (Mt in Jewish style uses the impersonal "theological" passive instead of the divine name [*GrBib* § 236]), no one would have escaped alive from this disaster. The narrative of Josephus does indeed indicate a terrible loss of life in the Palestinian Jewish community. That even a few escape is attributed

Book Five: Judea and Jerusalem (19:1—25:46)

to God's mercy toward "the chosen," that is, the Christian members of the Palestinian Jewish community.

In calling this the "end," Mt merges the historic and the apocalyptic. To understand his point of view we must remember that to the Palestinian Jewish Christian community, of which Mt is here the spokesman, the total collapse, as it seemed, of Palestinian Judaism was truly the end of their world. A world in which Yahweh was not worshiped by his people in his land in his Temple was not the world of history. No similar act of judgment was related in the OT; for there could be no messianic hope to survive this ruin—the Messiah had come and initiated the reign. This community was aware, perhaps better aware than Gentile Christians, of the magnitude of the historical and theological crisis of the fall of Palestinian Judaism. With the disaster a new phase of the reign began.

(e) False Messiahs (24:23–25)

These lines are a fuller doublet of 24:5, taken from another source. There are echoes in the NT of false prophets in the apostolic Church who cannot be positively identified, nor can the signs and wonders that are attributed to them. The disciples have been forewarned against such pretenders (cf. Mk 13:21–23).

(f) The Day of the Son of Man (24:26–28)

These lines are inserted from Q (Lk 17:23–24,37 par.) and do not belong in this context originally. The theme is related to the theme of the preceding lines. 26. *in the desert*: Christians need not go out into the desert to seek the Messiah, as some went out after Theudas, a messianic leader whose insurrection was suppressed by the procurator C. Cuspius Fadus (AD 44–46; cf. Josephus, *Ant.* 20.5, 1 § 97). Nor should they accept invitations to join secret meetings in inner chambers. 27. *as the lightning*: The coming of the Messiah will be as easy to see as the flash of lightning across the sky. 28. A proverb of cryptic meaning is cited; the gathering of vultures shows that there is carrion that attracts them, and the parousia of the Son of Man will be just as easily discerned.

(g) The Parousia of the Son of Man (24:29–31)

29. This verse is the sequel to 24:22. Mt has made the junction of history and eschatology even tighter by adding "immediately." He has expanded Mk's description of the parousia in 24:30–31. The parousia is described in terms largely taken from OT apocalyptic passages; for comparisons see Is 13:10, 34:4 (24:29); Zech 12:12–14 (24:30); Is 27:13; Zech 2:10 (24:31). It is influenced by the Son of Man epiphany in Dn 7:13–14. The cosmic disturbances are a conventional part of OT imagery when the approach of God's judgments are described. 30. *the sign of the Son of Man:* This is not clear. A sign from heaven is asked in 16:1–4, but Jesus denies that it will be given; this answer is not directed toward the eschatological event. The sign of the Son of Man may be identical with his epiphany "in power and great glory." Apocalyptic imagery, of course, should not be taken in a crass literal sense; what is described is a manifest vindication of the Son of Man as one endowed with power and glory and a gathering of his elect, expressed in language that suggests the OT theme of the ingathering of Israel. The eschatological essence of the event is that it is final. The coming of the Son of Man as Mt conceived it could easily be the establishment of the community of the Risen Son of Man as the new Israel after the destruction of the old Israel. This is not identical with the eschatological parousia, but it is an event that anticipates the parousia and moves closer to it.

(h) The Parable of the Fig Tree (24:32–33)

The blossoming of the fig tree occurs at the end of the rainy season and signifies that the dry season of summer is at hand. One may ask more precisely what are "all these things" that are to happen, and what is it that is "near, at the door." Although the saying has an eschatological intent, it does not seem to lie in its original context. In its present position, the coming of the Son of Man is the sign that the Son of Man is coming. The events that are the "beginnings of the pangs" indicate the catastrophe of Jerusalem, which is presented as one event with the parousia. Yet the "signs" of the end event are of such a general character that they can hardly furnish the kind of precise indication suggested here. Furthermore, there is a more than superficial lack of harmony between these lines and 24:34–36, which follow. The apostolic Church was alive with speculations about the parousia of which

BOOK FIVE: JUDEA AND JERUSALEM (19:1—25:46)

we have only traces; and these verses reflect some of these speculations, which could, of course, arrive at no certain conclusion (cf. Mk 13:28-29).

(i) The Time of the Parousia (24:34-36)

The speculations mentioned above are also reflected in these verses. The affirmation that "all these things" will happen in this generation is clear, and there is no reason to alter the meaning of the word "generation" from its usual sense except a fear that the Scriptures may be in error if it is not so altered. The sentence can be understood only in the light of that merging of history and eschatology upon which we have remarked above. 35. This saying may originally come from another context in which it serves as an asseveration of the statement that these events will come in this generation. 36. *nor the Son:* Yet what seems to be as clear an indication of time, apart from an exact date, as one could wish is followed by a statement that not even the Son knows the day and the hour. Distinctions between the fall of Jerusalem and the parousia have no basis in the text; and reservations on the ignorance of the Son likewise have no basis in the text. The words mean that Jesus did not know the time, and he did not add "in my human nature" or "with my experiential knowledge." Perhaps it would have made no sense had he added such phrases, but in this case it would have been better to omit a completely unnecessary remark. We are, of course, not dealing with "the very words" of Jesus; but it is hard to understand how the apostolic traditions would have preserved such a difficult saying if it did not rest on the memory of something Jesus had said. The first Christian writer to find this sentence difficult was Luke (21:32-33) and he solved his problem by omitting it. We cannot do this; and perhaps the only remark that can be made is that there is much about the relations of Jesus and the Father that we do not know.

Both Mk (13:33-37) and Lk (21:34-36) conclude the discourse at this point with an exhortation to watchfulness. Matthew has expanded the discourse by the use of the material in 24:37—25:46.

(j) Exhortations to Vigilance (24:37-41)

These sayings come from Q, but the forms they have in Mt and Lk (17:26-27, 34-35) exhibit variations. 37. *the days of Noah:* The warning about the deluge is significant; it does not say that men were sinning, but that they were engaged in innocent secular occupations. Their sin was to give no thought to impending catastrophe. The disciples are warned against that interest in secular business that makes them forget the parousia. The saying may originally have referred more precisely to the fall of Jerusalem rather than to the parousia. 40. The parousia will manifest the difference between men—a difference that is not now apparent. Two men plowing or two women grinding meal share the same occupation and look alike externally, but God knows the difference and will make it clear. The precise meaning of "taken" and "left" is not made clear, nor need it be. Those who are "taken" will be taken because they are ready; they have shown the vigilance that is recommended.

(k) The Prudent Householder (24:42–44)

The parable of vigilance occurs in variant forms (see Mk 13:33–37; Lk 12:39–40). The parable reinforces the uncertainty of the time of the parousia (see 24:34–36). 43. *the thief in the night*: It will come without warning, as the thief comes in the night; the same image is used in 1 Thes 5:2. *digs through*: The Palestinian house was often built entirely or partly of clay bricks. The parable clearly does not envisage signs by which the near approach of the parousia can be discerned.

(l) The Faithful and Prudent Servant (24:45–51)

This parable comes from Q, and Mt and Lk (12:42–46) are unusually close to each other. In Lk the parable is spoken in answer to a question of Peter; and although the parable is certainly eschatological, its primary reference is to those who have authority in the Church and are the stewards of the goods of the Church. 45. *set over his household*: It is their duty to dispense these goods, which are not their own but have been entrusted to them precisely so that they may be dispensed. 47. *set him over all his possessions*: The reward of fidelity in this is commitment of a greater trust. 48–49. Tyrannical treatment of those over whom one has the charge and the use of the goods for self-indulgence is infidelity in the commission. This is more than lack of vigilance; but the excuse for such conduct is the delay of the parousia. Let all know that the Lord will come when he is not expected. 51. *will punish him [or cut him in pieces]*: The punishment threatened to the unfaithful servant is dismemberment, a vigorous and to us disagreeable

Book Five: Judea and Jerusalem (19:1—25:46)

metaphor taken from the practices of the Hellenistic-Oriental world; after this the assignment of his lot with the hypocrites seems anticlimactic. The hypocrites are the same against whom the invective of ch. 23 is directed; the parable recognizes that the faults of Jewish religious leaders can be found also in Christian religious leaders. 51b. A tag of Mt (8:12; 13:42,50; 22:13).

(m) The Parable of the Wise and Foolish Virgins (25:1-13)

This parable, peculiar to Mt, has a remarkable combination of a homely scene with a tragic end. The point of the parable is foresight, not vigilance in the strict sense; all the girls sleep, five of them are ready. 1. *bridegroom*: Some mss. add "and the bride." There is a lack of detailed information about wedding practices in NT Judaism. There was certainly a solemn wedding procession from the home of the bride to the home of the bridegroom; the taking of the bride from her father's house to his own by the bridegroom was the symbolic act of marriage. The critical reading ("bridegroom" only) indicates that the bride's female attendants went to meet the bridegroom and his party and accompanied them to the house of the bride. Whether the wedding feast was held in the house of the bride's father or in the house of the bridegroom is not clear; but it is the wedding feast from which the foolish girls are excluded, and since the groom speaks it appears that his house is meant. The wedding ceremonies were held at night, and the bridal couple was accompanied by torches and lamps. 5. Obviously there was no set time for the bridegroom to appear, and provisions had to be made for a long delay. 10. The closing and barring of the house door was not a simple task, and it was not opened again except for a real emergency; guests who could not arrive in time for the feast could not expect to be admitted. The parable restates yet again the uncertainty of the time of the parousia and recommends constant alertness, not the calculation of the signs of the times. The conception of the Messianic era as a wedding festival appears also in 9:15; 22:1-14 (see Jn 3:29).

(n) The Parable of the Talents (25:14-30)

The parable comes from Q, but there are a number of differences in detail between Mt and Lk (19:12-27). The point of the parable, however, is the same in both, and it seems unnecessary to postulate different sources. The sum in Mt is much larger, but this scarcely touches the point. The slaves who trade with the money double the investment; the timid slave buries the sum in the earth (see 13:44). 19. *settled accounts:* The point is not the uncertainty of the time of the parousia but the reckoning that will be demanded. It is possible here also to discern that the original form of the parable was directed to the officers of the Church. 21. *will set you over much:* The reward of fidelity is again the commission of greater responsibility; the admission to the joy of the lord means that the slave is admitted to intimate association with the owner. 24. This verse, which should not be allegorized, does indicate that the owner is demanding; and this is indeed the point of the whole parable. The slave has lost nothing, but he has gained nothing. He could at least have invested the sum with moneylenders, who gave an excellent rate of interest in NT times. 28. *give it to him who has ten:* That the one talent is given to the slave who received ten is again not an allegorical feature; it affords room for the saying of v. 29. This paradoxical saying indicates that the powers conferred on the disciples grow with use and wither with disuse. The punishment for this type of infidelity is as severe as the punishment for more positive sins; it is expulsion into outer darkness, to which Mt has added the tag used in 24:51b.

(o) The Last Judgment (25:31–46)

This chapter in its present form has been produced by ecclesiastical expansions of sayings of Jesus. The usual designation of the passage as "The Last Judgment" is somewhat misleading; it is an imaginative scene in which is set the core of the moral teaching of Jesus. It has no parallel in the other Gospels. 32. The scene is the parousia, and "all nations" mean all mankind. But the process is addressed to the disciples; the standards on which they will be judged are set forth. That faith is not mentioned should lead to no theological conclusions; it is clear that for Mt as for other NT writers faith in Jesus is the first movement of man toward God. The point of this scene is that faith is not the whole movement; that it should transform the disciple. 32. *the sheep from the goats:* The separation of the sheep from the goats can be easily observed in modern Palestine when the time comes to transfer the animals to other pastures; sheep and goats feed together, but they are moved separately. 34. *the King:* Jesus is here given the title of king, unusual in the Gospels, and one of the signs of ecclesiastical expansion. *the kingdom:* This is not the reign that Jesus proclaimed but the eschatological kingdom; this is prepared "from the foundation of the world." In rabbinical theology

Book Five: Judea and Jerusalem (19:1—25:46)

the kingdom of the Messiah was one of the items created before the world. 35–36. The source of "the corporal works of mercy." Ministry to the basic needs of one's fellow man is the only canon of judgment mentioned here. One could paraphrase by saying that man is judged entirely on his behavior toward his fellow man. The evasion that this does not include man's duties toward God is met in this passage; Jesus identifies himself with those to whom service is given or refused, and their behavior toward men is their behavior toward God. The works mentioned are not those we usually call necessary works; and perhaps the word necessary is misleading here. The passage says nothing about what we would consider duties; man is judged on those things that he is accustomed not to consider duties. 44. *and did not minister to you:* The surprise of those who are condemned is easy to understand; they never accepted the fact that they encountered Jesus in other men and that they cannot distinguish between their duties to God and their duties to man. They are ranked with the devils, whose proper element is the fire of Gehenna. Eschatology means man is capable of a final decision that gives his life a permanent character. Both the righteous and the wicked here have made decisions that are irrevocable.

The position of this chapter in Mt at the conclusion of the final discourse of Jesus suggests that it is intended as the last word of Jesus to the disciples. The chapter is weighty theologically. Like the last discourse in Jn, the theme is love based on the identity of Jesus with men. In the last analysis, it is love that determines whether men are good or bad. If their love is active, failure to reach perfect morality in other ways will be rare, and it will be forgiven. But there is no substitute for active love.

Chapter 7

The Passion Narrative (26:1—27:66)

INTERPRETERS GENERALLY AGREE THAT this part of the Gospel tradition was the first part to acquire a fixed structure. No part of the life of Jesus is related in such detail and with such close agreement in the sources. The amount of space given to the passion in Mk as compared to the rest of his Gospel shows the place this narrative had in the apostolic Church; in Mt, the disproportion, although smaller, is still notable. The earliest proclamation of Jesus centered on the story of the death and the resurrection. This was the great saving act of God, the climax of the saving acts in the history of salvation. Paul said that he preached Christ and him crucified (1 Cor 2:2).

Mt's Passion Narrative shows a few expansions of his own. Some of these are legendary details, others come from a "fulfillment" interpretation of OT texts of a character similar to that observed frequently in the infancy narratives, less frequently elsewhere in the Gospels. It is not an account of the words of Jesus; although Jesus speaks more frequently in Mt than in Mk, he is generally silent. Strangely to us, the Gospels have no theological exposition of the passion, either through the words of Jesus or the words of others. This was left to the apostolic teaching, which we can see illustrated in the epistles of Paul.

The Passion Narrative was of all the portions of the Gospels certainly the first to be included in a liturgical recital as well as in the proclamation, and liturgical influences must have operated in the formation of the narrative. The detailed investigation of these traces is a work still to be done.

The Passion Narrative (26:1—27:66)

(A) The Conspiracy of the Jewish Authorities (26:1–5)

Matthew notably expands Mk (14:1–2) here. He connects this passage immediately with the preceding discourse. The prediction of Jesus, peculiar to Mt, is a solemn introduction to the narrative; the words give purpose and clarity to the sequence of events that were not realized by the disciples until after the resurrection. 2. *after two days:* This phrase, from Mk 14:1, has been given an entirely different force. The conspiracy also is described in an expanded form. The prediction of Jesus is balanced against the decision of the Jewish authorities; he knows what they are doing and is master of events. 3. *chief priests and elders:* These are the parties to the conspiracy (Mk, "chief priests and scribes"). "Chief priests" in the plural is not exact; there was only one "high priest," and the chief priests were the heads of the leading priestly families. *Caiaphas:* He is mentioned here only by Mt. Joseph Caiaphas was appointed high priest by the procurator Valerius Gratus in AD 18 and deposed by Vitellius in AD 36. He was the son-in-law of Annas, who controlled the priestly aristocracy for many years. 5. *not during the feast:* The desire that Jesus should not be killed on the feast leads to the question of the chronology of the crucifixion, which cannot be resolved here; but there seems to be no reason for the introduction of the phrase except to show that the conspiracy was frustrated in this detail. Jesus was certainly crucified during the Passover feast, which is what the conspirators wished to avoid. He is master of events.

(B) The Anointing at Bethany (26:6–13)

The story of the anointing appears in all four Gospels, and it is unlikely that such an incident occurred more than once. Lk places it earlier in the life of Jesus (7:36–50), does not name the host, and identifies the woman as a sinner. Jn places it before the passion (12:1–18), but locates it in the house of Martha and Mary at Bethany, and identifies the woman as Mary. Mt follows Mk; the host is Simon the leper (a difficult epithet, usually thought to identify him as one whom Jesus had healed), and the woman is neither named nor identified as a sinner. Jn also has substantially the same dialogue as Mk and Mt, but he identifies the complainer as Judas Iscariot. 7. Mt omits Mk's identification of the perfume as nard, but notes that it was expensive. To retain its fragrance, enough perfume for one application was sealed in small alabaster vases; it could be used only by breaking the vessel.

It was the custom to anoint the head generously at banquets; in Lk's account the host did not furnish ointment for Jesus. 8. *why this waste:* It was not the anointing but the costliness of the ointment to which "some"—probably the disciples—objected. 10. Jesus accepts the gesture in the spirit in which it was intended, although he was no more in favor of luxury than anyone else; and he excuses the extravagance by an allusion to his impending death and burial, which permits him to accept it. The narrative illustrates his graciousness in accepting a service he would never have accepted if he had first been asked, and he reads the disciples a lesson in the interpretation of motives. The gesture was foolish but generous; it is the only action in the Gospels that is promised a perpetual and universal memory. The exchange surely made a profound impression on those who witnessed it.

(C) The Treachery of Judas (26:14–16)

14. *then:* The adverb does not indicate any inner connection between the betrayal and the preceding event; Matthew uses such connecting particles throughout his account of the last days of Jesus and thus makes the events follow in rapid sequence. *Judas:* In all the Gospels the initiative comes from Judas. The Gospels do not always refrain from representing the inner thoughts of persons; Mk 14:4 in the preceding incident describes the objection that was thought but not expressed. But no Gospel attempts to probe the motivation of the most astounding act they relate, the betrayal of Jesus by one of the Twelve. Speculations are numerous, but here they seem useless. 15. *thirty silver coins:* Only Mt specifies the amount (30 [silver shekels]). The number comes not from tradition but from Zech 11:12, and Zech in turn probably alludes to Ex 21:32, in which damages for the life of a slave killed by a goring ox are set at 30 silver shekels. Certainly there were difficulties in apprehending Jesus that the Gospels have not set forth fully; the priests were ready to accept help in doing it clandestinely, but this is not altogether easy to combine with the public display they not only permitted but encouraged. The phrases used both here and in 26:4 suggest assassination rather than a judicial process. There were no doubt varied counsels in the priestly ruling class on how to deal with the matter.

The Passion Narrative (26:1—27:66)

(D) The Preparation for the Passover (26:17-19)

A night elapses between the anointing at Bethany and the preparation of the Passover. In the Syn the last dinner is a Passover dinner. 17. *on the first day of matzoth:* The phrase is somewhat imprecise. Matthew's abbreviation of Mk is startling here; he omits all reference to the man carrying the pitcher and the implications of second sight possessed by Jesus and gives a narrative that supposes that arrangements with someone (whose name he does not give) have been previously made for the use of his house for the Passover dinner. Such reserve is not characteristic of Matthew; there can be no reason for his omission except that he saw nothing extraordinary in the incident reported in Mk.

(E) The Traitor (26:20-25)

20. *reclined:* Jews of NT times had adopted the Hellenistic practice of reclining around the table on couches. In Mt and Mk it is at the very beginning of the meal that Jesus chose to reveal the treachery of one of the company; Lk postpones the announcement until after the Eucharistic words. Jn also puts it early, but solves the problem by sending Judas out of the room after the announcement. 21. *one of you will betray me:* That this news cast gloom over the assembly is not surprising; and this is a better argument than most for proposing that the announcement of the betrayal at this point is a later expansion. That each of the disciples should ask seriously whether he was the traitor would exhibit a surprising insecurity, and this also points to a period of reflection when the Church came to realize that each of its members carries potential treachery within him. The answer of Jesus does not identify the traitor. 23. *dipped in the dish:* The dinner was served in large bowls, set in the succession of courses in the center of the group; each reached into the bowl for a morsel. In Jn (13:26) this custom leads to the identification of Judas by a morsel that Jesus hands to him. To eat together and share the same bowl denotes fellowship; and the contrast of fellowship and treachery is heightened by that act that negates the community of those who eat together. 24. *had he not been born:* The condemnation of the act of Judas is the most severe in all the Gospels; the death of Jesus is inevitable, "as it is written," but it is not inevitable that one of his disciples should betray him. 25. *is it I?:* Matthew adds an expansion of his own in which Jesus

expressly discloses to Judas alone that he knows who the traitor is; this is a step in the development that is completed in the account in Jn.

(F) The Institution of the Eucharist (26:26–29)

Paul has the earliest of the formulas in which the institution of the Eucharist is preserved (1 Cor 11:23–25). The variations between Paul and Lk (22:15–20) on the one hand, and Mt and Mk (14:22–25) on the other, should not be exaggerated; but the texts do vary. That this passage was a liturgical text is certain, and thus it was assured a relatively fixed form very early. Mt follows Mk closely with only one major expansion (in v. 28). Verse 29 suggests a reference to the last cup of the Passover dinner. 26. All three Syn mention the blessing, the breaking, and the distribution; Mt adds the unnecessary command to eat. *this is my body:* Here without any modification; but Paul and Lk add, "which is for you." 27. Mt also adds the command to drink; Mk has the simple indicative ("they drank"). 28. *this is my blood of the covenant:* Paul and Lk have "This cup is the new covenant in my blood." The formula of Mt and Mk is more explicitly sacramental than that of Paul and Lk. The "blood of the covenant" is an allusion to Ex 24:4–8, where the covenant between Yahweh and Israel is concluded with the offering of sacrifice. The blood of the victims, sprinkled on the altar, which symbolizes Yahweh, and on the elders, who represent the people of Israel, signifies the community of the two parties in the covenant. The blood of Jesus likewise, which means his death, is the effective symbol of the community that he establishes between the Father and men. *is shed for many:* For all without restriction. *for the remission of sins:* Only Mt adds the phrase that expresses more clearly the effect of the reconciling death. Certain Israelite sacrifices atoned for sin and guilt, by which were meant ritual offenses. The atoning death of Jesus liberates man not only from ritual sin and guilt, but from sin simply, for which there was no atonement in the Israelite sacrificial system. 29. *when I drink it anew with you:* This is the final cup Jesus shares with his disciples; he will not drink with them again until they meet in the Messianic banquet (see 8:11). Mt and Mk do not have the precept to repeat the act, but nothing suggests that they diverged from the practice of the apostolic Church. The Eucharistic meal celebrated in the Church was an anticipation of the Messianic banquet (26:29), and the belief that Jesus was present to share the meal was implicit in the idea of the Messianic banquet. (See P. Benoit, "The Holy Eucharist," *Scr* 8 [1956] 97–108; 9 [1957] 1–14.)

The Passion Narrative (26:1—27:66)

(G) The Prediction of Peter's Denial (26:30-35)

Mt follows Mk (14:26-31) closely with a few expansions of no special significance. 30. *a hymn*: Sung to conclude the dinner, this would have been Ps 114/5-118, the second part of the Hallel. Considering Jesus has spent the preceding nights in Bethany, there was nothing remarkable in the journey of the group to the Mt. of Olives; because Jesus had traversed this path nightly, it was possible for Judas to tell the priests where he could be apprehended with no disturbance. 31. But while only one betrays, all the others will be offended by him this very night; he will disappoint their messianic hopes. *for it is written*: The text is an inexact quotation of Zech 13:7, but the point is not lost; the group will be helpless when they lose the leadership of Jesus. 32. They will not see him again until they go to Galilee after the resurrection. Mt has an apparition in Galilee, but Mk does not.

33. Attention is again drawn to Peter, who speaks now for himself and not for the group; Mt expands the words of Peter's asseveration. But Peter's excessive self-confidence will be followed by a fall more grievous than the fall of the others; the rest will be offended, but Peter will deny Jesus, and that this very night, "before cockcrow," that is, before dawn. 35. Not only Peter but the others join in affirming their loyalty. Certainly one of the most indelible memories of the group of disciples was their breakdown at the time of the passion, and they told this part of the story without sparing details or persons. It was an expression of their awareness that in the disciple infidelity lies always very close to the surface.

(H) Gethsemane (26:36-46)

Mt still follows Mk (14:32-42) closely with amplifications in small details. This is one of the most remarkable scenes of the Gospels, and it has been pointed out that the witnesses—according to their own testimony—slept through it and that they must therefore have reconstructed the incident. But this is hypercritical. The incident shows that Jesus was under severe emotional strain comparable to nothing else in the Gospels, and that once in his life he sought the help of others. These things could be observed; and the reconstruction of the memory is built upon these observations.

36. *Gethsemane [oil press]*: An olive grove grew on the western slope of the Mt. of Olives near Jerusalem. It is not certain whether the modern grove that bears the name is the same site, but it lies in the immediate area.

38. Jesus openly confessed his agitation and asked that the disciples remain awake with him; he does not tell them what they are awaiting. The words are addressed to Peter, James, and John, who also witnessed the transfiguration (17:1–8), and only they could attest anything about the prayer. 39. The narrative supposes that Jesus spoke distinctly enough to be audible at a short distance. *if it be possible:* The prayer expresses a repugnance for the experience of the passion; the Gospels report only what could be seen and heard and do not attempt to analyze the thoughts and feelings of Jesus, and the modern commentator will do well to follow their example. 40. The words in which Jesus asks for the companionship of the disciples are loosely adopted from Ps 42:6; this is derived from Mk. In keeping with Matthew's usual treatment of Peter, he is the one being addressed, not the disciples. 41. Matthew has altered the form of the prayer slightly and has repeated it a second time. *to enter into temptation:* Not merely to experience temptation in our sense of the word but "temptation" as it is meant in the Lord's Prayer (6:13): a difficulty that one does not overcome. "Spirit" and "flesh" are a common biblical antithesis, used frequently in the Pauline epistles. The spirit is not merely the internal psychic principles of man, but the psychic principles strengthened by a divine impulse. Even with the divine impulse, the "flesh," which means man in his concrete existence, is not able to sustain "temptation" in the biblical sense of the word.

45. The disciples were too weary to remain awake; men rose and retired early in the ancient world, and no one here remains awake except Jesus and the arresting party. Most interpreters see a gentle irony in the permission to sleep that Jesus grants; it is now unimportant whether the disciples remain awake or not. 46. There is a certain incoherence in the permission to sleep followed immediately by the command to arise. This incoherence no doubt reflects the confused memories of the disciples, who doze in a manner that makes them half-aware of what is going on, and who are suddenly aroused to the greatest catastrophe in their experience. Jesus himself saw the approaching party; the Passover falls during the full moon, and the party no doubt carried torches.

(I) The Arrest of Jesus (26:47–56)

Mt still follows Mk (14:43–52) except for some minor abbreviations and two notable expansions. 47. *Judas:* He is mentioned as if he were the leader of the party, but this is unlikely. Judas knew where Jesus should be sought,

The Passion Narrative (26:1—27:66)

at least in what neighborhood. That he should bring the party immediately to the very spot seems astonishing; this detail can probably be attributed to the confused recollections of an exciting and confused evening. **48.** *the one I kiss:* The kiss, a normal form of greeting, was necessary to identify the person whom the party sought in the darkness illuminated only by the full moon and the torches. Jesus was not that well known to the arresting party, and the priests had no desire to apprehend the whole group. **50.** *why are you here:* The first of Mt's expansions is a response of Jesus to the greeting of Judas. Tradition was not satisfied with the silence recorded in Mk; Lk (22:48) has another variation of the response of Jesus, and Jn (18:4–8) makes the signal of Judas entirely unnecessary. Modern interpreters (against most Eng translations) take the words of Jesus as an elliptical imperative, rather than a question: "Friend, for what you have come!" meaning, "Do the business for which you have come." **51.** *cut off his ear:* The disciple who offered resistance is named only in Jn (18:10) as Peter; Jn also names the slave. Matthew's usual interest in Peter suggests that neither he nor Mark had this bit of information. *the slave of the high priest:* He may have been the leader of the party. The arresting group is unsatisfactorily described as "a crowd" by Mk, which Mt makes "a large crowd" (26:47), sent by the priests and elders (Mk adds "the scribes"). This is equivalent to saying that they did not know who the party were. The Temple had its own police, and since the priests were the chief actors in the passion, the Temple police were probably sent on this mission; it is unlikely that it was merely a mob. **52–54.** Mt's second expansion contains the response of Jesus to the attempt to defend him. The response is probably composed of sayings taken in part from other contexts, particularly the proverb of 52a. But the sharp rejection of the use of arms is entirely in accord with the teaching and the practice of Jesus; and no one else is said to intervene in a scene that would certainly have led to massive violence if some one had not stopped it. **52b.** The rejection of the use of arms is general, not a remark adapted to this particular situation; it condemns the use of arms as futile rather than as immoral. **53.** *twelve legions of angels:* If Jesus wished or needed this type of help, it was available in far greater strength than the disciples could furnish. **54.** But if resistance is offered, the Scriptures will not be fulfilled; the reign of God will not be established in that way in which God intends. That there can ever be other situations in which the reign will be advanced by the use of arms is not denied by this saying; but the saying lends little support to such an understanding of the reign.

55. The words of Jesus to the crowd show that he freely surrenders himself. They need not have sought him out in a lonely place when he was within easy reach in the very Temple precincts. That the Jewish leaders did not desire a public arrest is a constant theme in the Passion Narrative; and this is revealing about public sentiment toward Jesus. For the same reason there is no mention of the invocation of Roman authority at this stage of the passion; the Gospel tradition is clear that the arrest was the act of Jewish religious leaders.

For the rest of the Passion Narrative the disciples were not eyewitnesses, but there was no difficulty in reconstructing events that occurred in the presence of large numbers of people. The disciples were ready to defend Jesus by force; when he himself rejected defense, they did not know what to do.

(J) Jesus Before the Council (26:57-75)

The arresting party led Jesus to the house of the high priest. Here the council (Sanhedrin) was assembled, composed of 72 members drawn from the priests, the scribes, and the elders. That the house of the high priest, however large it was, could seat this assembly seems unlikely. 57. *Caiaphas*: The name does not appear in Mk (cf. 26:3; but also Jn 18:13). 59. *false testimony*: Mt condenses Mk's account of the witnesses, but the sources are at one that the witnesses were perjured and even then could not reach a satisfactory agreement on their testimony. The testimony on which two witnesses agreed is reported in a saying in Jn 2:19, the only place in the Gospels where anything remotely resembling the charge is found. Two witnesses were the necessary minimum for a condemnation. As the story proceeds the two witnesses did not support the charge, and the high priest then puts Jesus under an oath to answer a direct question. The charge concerning the Temple was blasphemy against the Temple; see Jer 26:1-19, where Jeremiah was threatened with death for a prediction that the Temple would be destroyed. 62-63. The question of the high priest is a question concerning the messianic claims of Jesus; but the formula "the Messiah, the son of God" should probably be regarded as a Christian rather than a Jewish formula. This raises a critical problem concerning the charge on which Jesus was convicted. 64. The answer of Jesus combines two messianic texts, Ps 110:1 and Dn 7:13; by the use of these texts Jesus declares himself the king Messiah and the Son of Man. That this claim should be treated as

The Passion Narrative (26:1—27:66)

blasphemy has long been a problem. *you have said it:* This must have been in Matthew's mind equivalent to Mk's "I am" (14:62); the use of the two OT texts is certainly a clear affirmation. But we have nothing in Jewish sources to suggest that a claim of messiahship was regarded as a blasphemy, even if the claim were proved false. 65. The claim is here immediately taken as a capital crime. The rending of one's garments was an ancient token of grief; in Pharisaic Judaism it was a sign of grief at seeing or hearing of some grievous violation of the Law. 67. The rough treatment to which Jesus is subjected following the sentence is not attributed to any group in particular. Mt's amplification of the taunt in which Jesus is challenged to prophesy gives point to the taunt; Jesus was among strangers.

This trial is one of the most complex problems in Gospel interpretation. See further J. Blinzler, *The Trial of Jesus* (Westminster, 1959); P. Winter, *On the Trial of Jesus* (SPB 1; Berlin, 1961); K. H. Schelkle, *Die Passion Jesu* (Heidelberg, 1949); E. Lohse, *Die Geschichte des Leidens und Sterbens Jesu Christi* (Gütersloh, 1964). The problem is not simplified by the fact that Mt 27:1 (like Mk 15:1) follows immediately after 26:56 (Mk 14:51 par.). It has often been noticed that the process deviates in many ways from the standards of legal process set down in the Talmud. The Talmud is a post-Christian collection that is not always valid for the practices of NT times; and in describing the legal process of the council, the Talmud describes an institution that was extinct after AD 70. But it can and does preserve some genuine historical memories. As the trial is described there was no effort whatever to maintain a just process; but until the contrary is clearly proved it should be assumed that the council would adhere to legal forms, and that all the more closely in a case the verdict of which was prearranged.

In addition there is the problem of a certain lack of coherence in the narrative, noted above. It appears that the testimony of blasphemy against the Temple would have been a better charge for the purpose of the council than the charge of blasphemy for messianic claims, and it should not have been too difficult to arrange a harmonious testimony; one has the impression that the competence of the priests has strangely broken down. That the accused should be put under oath to make a statement by which he could be condemned is a strange procedure that has never been satisfactorily explained.

For these reasons, the hypothesis that the night trial scene is a theological recital rather than a historical account should be considered. The purpose of the recital is not to charge the council with perversion of justice;

this charge is abundantly clear already. Its purpose is to set forth the real reason why Jesus was condemned to death by the Jewish leaders. The real reason, whatever the alleged reasons, was that he claimed to be and was their king Messiah and the Son of Man. The question of Caiaphas and the answer of Jesus are both couched in terms of the Christian profession of faith. When the Jewish leaders encountered their Messiah and refused to believe in him, they could do nothing else but remove him.

69. To this recital is attached the story of the denial of Peter, which is independent of it; the denial represented as occurring at the court of the high priest, the open space around which the house was built. Thus far Peter could follow Jesus with some safety. The threefold denial occurs as predicted with some modifications in detail. Mk attributes the first denial to the teasing of a slave girl; Mt introduces a second slave girl and specifies how it was that Peter was recognized as a Galilean. Dialectal differences were numerous in ancient Palestine, as they are in the modern Arabic spoken in Palestine. No explanation of the failure of Peter's courage in such hostile territory is necessary. 75. Both Mt and Lk add "bitterly" to the statement that Peter wept. The lapse of the Rock of the apostolic group was remembered because it was such a striking demonstration of common human weakness; but it was also remembered because Peter neither concealed nor excused his lapse. For such lapses there is no remedy but repentance.

(K) Jesus Delivered to Pilate (27:1-2)

Matthew has rewritten Mk 15:1a. somewhat extensively, but he leaves Mk 15:lb (Mt 27:2 par.) almost unchanged. The purpose of the rewriting in 27:1 is to make more coherent the transition from the night session to the morning session. Hence he adds the explicit purpose "to kill him." Lk has handled the problem more radically by placing the interrogatory process in the morning session. We have noticed that Mt 27:1 and Mk 15:1 can be read immediately after Mt 26:56 and Mk 14:51. 2. Mt alone adds the title of Pilate, Gk *hēgemōn*, Lat *procurator*. This officer was a subordinate of the provincial governor (Lat *legatus*) in the Roman system of provincial administration. In the provinces the right of passing a capital sentence (Lat *ius gladii*) was reserved to the Roman authority.

The Passion Narrative (26:1—27:66)

(L) The Death of Judas Iscariot (27:3-10)

This passage is peculiar to Mt. There is another tradition of the death of Judas in Acts 1:18-19 which shows definite variations; Judas there purchases the field himself, and he dies by a fall and not by suicide. Both passages are better understood as legendary material about the death of Judas. **4-5.** The remorse of Judas and his throwing the money into the Temple are vividly and dramatically described. We do not know of any prohibition that disallowed putting such money into the Temple treasury. **8.** *field of Blood:* In Gk *hakeldamach* (Aram *hᵃqel dᵉmā* [Bl-Deb-F § 39, 3]); see Acts 1:19. That there was such a burying ground near Jerusalem must be assumed, and it is very probable that the name was connected by Jewish Christians with the legend of Judas. **9.** The quotation of Zech 11:12-13 under the attribution of Jer is a celebrated problem; it is also one of the most striking examples of "fulfillment" texts in Mt. The text is not quoted exactly from either the MT or the LXX, although had it been, the passage would have been more pointed. The use of the text hinges on an ancient variation. Where the MT twice reads "potter," the LXX reads much more probably "treasury." In this respect the quotation follows the MT rather than the LXX; and it is not impossible that the source of the quotation was aware of the wordplay (treasury, *'ôṣār*; potter, *yôṣēr*). Yet the form of 27:10 suggests the story of Acts 1:18 rather than the story of Mt. In the story of Mt, Judas fulfills the text in both readings. The attribution to Jer is credited by most scholars to Mt's source and possibly to a florilegium of texts, but it seems unlikely that a florilegium would have circulated with this attribution. Some scholars see an allusion to the purchase of a field in Jer 32:6-15 and to Jeremiah's visit to the potter in Jer 18:2-3, from which allusions the entire text is attributed to Jer. This seems unlikely; and it is more probable that the source, which quoted from memory, attributed the passage to Jer by unconscious association of the text with these passages of Jer.

(M) The Hearing Before Pilate (27:11-14)

Mt here follows Mk (15:2-5) closely with only verbal modifications; the addition of the elders to the priests as accusers (27:12) is not significant. **11.** *are you the king of the Jews:* The charge of claiming kingship is introduced abruptly, and it was not a part of the account of the night hearing; again we encounter a certain lack of consistency in the traditions about the trial. This must have been the charge laid by the accusers, but the narratives do not say so explicitly. The answer of Jesus, like his answer in 26:64, is noncommittal; he neither accepts nor denies the charge. Jn, in which the theme of kingship is much more prominent in the Passion Narrative, adds an explanation of the nature of the kingship of Jesus (18:33–37). 13. *how many things:* What these things were of which the priests and the elders accused him is not stated. It is quite possible that the early Church saw in the silence of Jesus a fulfillment of Is 53:7; but if this awareness were deep when Mt was written, one would expect another fulfillment text. The charge of claiming the kingship of the Jews was a charge of treason against the authority of Rome. Pilate obviously did not take the charge seriously. Jewish messianic insurrections in Palestine were dealt with severely by the Roman authorities.

(N) The Sentence of Death (27:15–26)

Matthew's modifications of Mk (15:6–15) are again merely modal. He omits Mk 15:7b, the details of the crimes of Barabbas, expands Mk 15:11–14 (27:20–23 par.), the dialogue of Pilate and the Jewish leaders, and adds two episodes of his own, the dream of Pilate's wife (27:19) and Pilate's symbolic washing of the hands (27:24–25). 15. The custom of an amnesty at Passover is not elsewhere attested, but such a practice was not foreign to Roman policy in the provinces, and similar practices are attested for other territories. The narrative supposes that the selection is made by popular petition, and Pilate seeks to direct the petition to Jesus. 16. *Barabbas:* Described by Mk as a revolutionary, one of the party of the Zealots. The play on his name is evident; *Bar-'abbā* in Aramaic means "son of the father," and he is chosen in preference to Jesus, the true son. The play on the name is not a sufficient reason for calling the Barabbas episode legend or midrash. 19. The story of the wife of Pilate, on the other hand, must be characterized as legend. The dream motif occurs also in the infancy narratives of Mt (1:20; 2:12,13,19). The Gentile woman learns by revelation that Jesus is a "righteous man"; in the context the word would mean no more than innocent, but the OT echoes of the word are clearly audible. 20. Mt here as earlier adds the elders to the priests as accusers; their work is now to persuade those who had come to petition for the amnesty to select Barabbas.

What follows is not the description of a legal process. There is no further hearing, no interrogation of witnesses. The sentence is implied in 27:26. That there was a process must be assumed, but this was not

The Passion Narrative (26:1—27:66)

something tradition described in detail. The important factor was not the process, but the pressure that determined the outcome of the process. The traditions clearly affirm that Pilate knew that there was no genuine charge against Jesus. Matthew's addition of the symbolic washing of the hands emphasizes this. The traditions do not flatter Pilate in this respect; he who condemns an innocent man under pressure is morally not very far above those who put on the pressure. 25. *all the people answered*: Matthew's addition of the acceptance by the Jewish spokesmen of the guilt is a theological addition, written with the disaster of the Jewish War in mind; this was seen by the early Christians as a terrible judgment on the people who had secured the killing of their Messiah by the perversion of justice (see further J. A. Fitzmyer, *TS* 26 [1965] 667–71). It is scarcely Matthew's thought that the plea of innocence that he puts in the mouth of Pilate (27:24) could be regarded as genuine.

Historians have noticed that no process is described and that the career of Pilate as described by Josephus is not in harmony with this picture of a man who easily yields to popular pressure. On this basis a number of scholars have argued that the Gospel traditions have transferred the responsibility for the death of Jesus from the Romans to the Jews, who in this hypothesis had no part in the process. To remove the Jewish leaders from the narrative of the passion is effectively to deny that we have any history of the passion at all. We do have a history, popular as its character may be, and in this history Jews and the Roman authorities both collaborate in the execution of Jesus. In the simplified Gospel narrative it is very likely that the attitude of Pilate has been softened. Pilate would have been ready to accept the charge that Jesus was a revolutionary; the story of his administration as related by Josephus shows that he was extremely harsh toward revolutionary movements. The Jewish leaders laid the charge against Jesus, and Pilate found little difficulty in accepting the charge. The purpose of the form that the Gospel narrative takes at this point is not to absolve Pilate of guilt but to affirm the legal innocence of Jesus in terms of Roman law as well as in terms of Jewish law.

26. The scourging was regularly inflicted in the Roman process before execution by crucifixion. The Gospels (except Lk) mention it casually, and although a scourging could be a dreadful process, they do not suggest that it was other than routine.

(O) The Mocking of the Soldiers (27:27–31)

The scene of this episode, the *praetorium*, was the official residence of the Roman governor who had the rank of praetor; Pilate did not have this rank, but *praetorium* had come to mean "headquarters." Opinion is divided whether Pilate resided at the Fortress Antonia, at the NW corner of the Temple area, or at the Herodian palace, the site of which was occupied by the police station of recent Jordanian Jerusalem (see P. Benoit, *Exégèse et théologie* [Paris, 1961] 1, 316–39). At full strength the cohort numbered 600 men, but it seems improbable that the entire force was gathered there. 28. *scarlet cloak*: Matthew has changed the "purple" of Mk to a scarlet cloak. Purple (the celebrated Phoenician dye) was the color of royalty and of the Roman aristocracy; the cloak of the Roman soldier was scarlet, and Matthew's change is no doubt correct. *crown of thorns*: It could not have been woven in a wreath. The long thorns used for fires would have been stored in the courtyard, and they could easily be arranged in a radiate crown of the type worn by Hellenistic kings (and familiar to us from its appearance on the Statue of Liberty). 29. *hail, King of the Jews*: The crude sport of the soldiers expresses their contempt not only for the alleged king but also for the people whose king this was supposed to be. In the Gospel traditions the scene had a mysterious significance. Jesus is acclaimed as king at the time when he fulfills his kingly duty, which is to save his people by his own death. It is only in the passion narratives and the infancy narratives of Mt and Lk that the theme of kingship appears in the Syn.

(P) The Way of the Cross (27:32)

The sons of Simon must have been members of the Roman church, and Mk mentions their name; but they were not known to Mt, who omits them. The Roman military had the right of impressing anyone for forced labor. What was carried was not the cross but the transverse beam; the upright stake was a permanent fixture at the place of execution. If Golgotha is to be identified with the site of the Church of the Holy Sepulcher, the distance was not long either from Antonia or from the Herodian palace.

The Passion Narrative (26:1—27:66)

(Q) The Crucifixion (27:33-44)

In spite of the innumerable references in Christian literature and art to the hill of Calvary, the site is nowhere described as a hill in the Gospels. It is now sufficiently well established that the site of the Church of the Holy Sepulcher lay outside the 1st-cent. wall of Jerusalem; but this of itself does not authenticate the site. 33. *Golgotha*: Interpreted in all three Syn as "skull," it comes from an Aram word, *gulgultā*. 34. *wine*: The drink offered Jesus is changed in Mt from Mk's "wine flavored with myrrh" to "wine mixed with gall," an allusion to Ps 69:22. It was the practice of Jewish women to offer a strong narcotic drink to men condemned to execution; Jesus refused this. 35. No details are given concerning the crucifixion. This was not a Roman punishment but an Oriental punishment adopted by the Romans. It was prohibited by Roman law to crucify Roman citizens; and normally crucifixion was used only for slaves, bandits, and rebels. The crucifixion of Jesus with two bandits shows the charge on which Jesus was condemned by Pilate. The division of the garments was a privilege of the squad of soldiers who handled the execution; the crucified were stripped entirely nude. Christian tradition saw here a fulfillment of Ps 22:19, quoted in all the Gospels. 37. *the title*: Affixed to the cross of the criminal was his charge; it indicated that Jesus had attempted to establish himself as king. 39. The mockery of those executed has been a universal feature wherever public executions have been practiced. The taunts are attributed to those who chanced to pass by and to the priests and scribes; Mt adds the elders, as usual. The taunts reflect the Messianic character of Jesus and the charge that he had threatened to destroy the Temple (26:61). 40. Mt has added "son of God" and "king of Israel" to the taunts mentioned by Mk. Mt 27:43 is added from Ps 22:9. 42. *he saved others but cannot save himself*: This taunt is an expression of the faith of the primitive Christians that this was the supreme saving act of Jesus. He is now the Messiah at the moment when he is jeered for failing to show what the Jews believed to be the Messianic qualities.

(R) The Death of Jesus (27:45-56)

Mt and Lk have omitted Mk's note of the third hour (midmorning) as the hour of crucifixion (Mk 15:25), but have retained the sixth hour (noon) and the ninth hour (midafternoon). The darkness that covered the land is a legendary feature in Mk; no explanation is offered, and the word does not mean a heavy overcast. It is a symbol of "the hour of darkness" (Lk 22:53). **46.** *Eli, Eli, . . . :* The words of Jesus are quoted from Ps 22:2, the opening line. This Ps, already cited, was used by the early Church as a Ps of the passion; it is as such a prophecy that it is used here, and not as a cry of interior abandonment expressed by Jesus. Mt quotes the psalm partly in Hebrew and partly in Aramaic. **47.** The bystander who recognized the name Elijah can hardly have been one of the soldiers. **48.** The drink offered Jesus was sour wine or wine vinegar, a cheap, thirst-quenching drink used by the poor; it was not unpalatable when mixed with water. Jesus was offered a share of the drink the soldiers no doubt carried with them. The tradition saw here another fulfillment of Ps 69:22. The loud cry uttered by Jesus is inarticulate in Mt and Mk.

51–53. Mt has a number of legendary features peculiar to itself. The veil of the temple divided the Holy Place from the Most Holy Place, accessible only to the high priest; Mk and Mt mean that the Most Holy Place at this moment ceases to be holy. The earthquake in the poetry of the OT is the tread of Yahweh's footsteps. The holy men who were buried in Jerusalem rise at the saving act of the Messiah; they recognize him, but Israel of the flesh does not. Even the centurion and the soldiers profess their belief that Jesus is the Son of God; this is a Christian formula of faith, and it is anticipated in the mouths of these Gentiles. Mt makes the confession a result of the signs; Mk, somewhat more impressively, presents it as the result of their witness of the death of Jesus. **55.** The women who had followed Jesus and served him in Galilee are mentioned in anticipation of the Resurrection Narrative. Mk mentions Mary of Magdala, Mary the mother of James (the Less) and Joses, and Salome. Mt mentions the two Marys (Joses must be the same as Joseph) and the mother of the sons of Zebedee, who need not be the same as Salome. This is the first time these names occur in Mt and Mk; and romantic identifications of them with nameless women mentioned earlier in the Gospels remain romantic. Mk mentions "many others" besides; Mt omits this.

(S) The Burial of Jesus (27:57–61)

Mt has abbreviated Mk (15:42–47) by omitting the detail of Pilate's surprise that Jesus had died; crucifixion was a slow death that sometimes took two or even three days. **43.** *Joseph of Arimathea:* Mt designates him "a rich man" instead of a respected member of the Jewish council; he has also made

Joseph a disciple instead of one "who expected the reign of God." But the term in Mk indicates one who looked for the true reign and not for the spurious messianism of the Pharisees, the Sadducees, or the Zealots. Mt may have seen a problem in the discipleship of a member of the council that had voted the death of Jesus. Arimathea is identified with the modern Rentis, about 20 mi. NE of Jerusalem. 60. *laid it in his own tomb*: The burial took place on the eve of the Sabbath; Mt and Mk describe a simple enveloping of the body in a new linen shroud. The tomb belonged to Joseph; it was a rock-cut tomb of a type very common in the vicinity of Jerusalem. The circular stone that was rolled in front of the entrance was used on some 1st-cent. tombs, which can still be seen. 61. It was not unimportant that the two Marys took careful note of the location of the tomb. The areas surrounding the walls of Jerusalem had literally hundreds, if not thousands of tombs, and the resurrection apologetic demanded that the spot where Jesus had been buried should be known exactly. For the same purpose it was important that the tomb was new, not previously used.

(T) The Guard at the Tomb of Jesus (27:62–66)

This passage is peculiar to Mt; it seems to be based on a local tradition, which is not without problems for interpreters. The following day here can be only the Sabbath, the day after the death of Jesus. 62. It is remarkable that the priests and the Pharisees show such an accurate knowledge of the prediction of a resurrection the disciples seem to have forgotten completely. 65. It is also somewhat remarkable that Pilate so readily granted a guard for a purpose he could only have thought to be absurd. Most remarkable is that this more than trivial detail of the resurrection apologetic is unknown to the other three Gospels. What can be concluded from the story is that the Jews charged the disciples with the theft of the body of Jesus. What can also be concluded is that Jews and disciples both agreed that the body of Jesus was missing from the tomb on the third day.

Chapter 8

The Resurrection Narrative (28:1-20)

IN THIS CONCLUDING NARRATIVE of the Gospels it is impossible to speak of a harmony of the Gospels. Each of the four Gospels goes its own way; even the correspondence between Mk 16:1–8, Mt 28:1–10, and Lk 24:1–11 is less close than usual, and Mk possibly ends at 16:8. Thereafter each Gospel has collected separate traditions. Evidently the Resurrection Narrative was not fixed in the way that the Passion Narrative and the Syn tradition of the life of Jesus was fixed. In addition, there is an allusion in 1 Cor 15:6 to an apparition that has no clear parallel in the Syn or in Jn. That the apostolic Church made no effort to harmonize these divergent and even conflicting accounts is of itself extremely significant; the faith in the resurrection did not depend on the fact that everyone had the same story. Nor should too much be made of the divergence; the resurrection is the most unique and shattering of all the events related in the Gospels, and confusion in the details is rather to be expected. Nor does the admixture of some legendary details have anything to do with the faith in the resurrection.

(A) The Empty Tomb (28:1-10)

Matthew seems to use Mk here, but his rewriting and additions are extensive. Mt says nothing of the women's purpose of anointing the body with spices; in Mk this is the motive for their visit to the tomb. The number of women is reduced from three to two. 1. The time is dawn on the day after the Sabbath; Mt's opening phrase means "after the Sabbath," not "on the evening of the Sabbath." 2–4. In Mt it is unnecessary for the women to ask

The Resurrection Narrative (28:1-20)

who shall remove the stone; Mt's legendary expansion makes them witnesses of the removal of the stone by an angel. The guards Mt has placed at the tomb are completely overcome by the apparition. Mt calls the being "the angel of the Lord" (see comment on 1:20); Mk and Lk more cautiously speak of "a youth" and "two men," but the description of their white garb and their luminous appearance is the same, and no doubt is left that celestial messengers are meant. The women are called to witness the vital fact that the tomb is empty. 7. The messenger commissions them to inform the disciples; Mt omits special mention of Peter. Both Mk and Mt, in contrast to Lk and Jn, record apparitions to the disciples located only in Galilee. For obvious reasons Mt changes Mk's note that the women told no one that they went to tell the disciples. Mt does not relate that they made their report; the apparition of Jesus himself completes the Resurrection Narrative. 9–10. Peculiar to Mt; but there are resemblances between this episode and the apparition of Jesus to Mary Magdalene in Jn 20:14–18. The words of Jesus are very close to the words of the angel in 28:7, and the two verses are very probably variations of the one saying.

(B) The Bribing of the Guard (28:11–15)

This section, peculiar to Mt, completes 27:62–66. It is remarkable that the guards should report to the priests instead of to their commanding officer. The purpose of the narrative is to explain the current story that the disciples stole the body. It is even explained how the guards could give this explanation and escape punishment for dereliction of duty.

(C) The Apostolic Commission (28:16–20)

This passage also is peculiar to Mt. 16. No mountain has previously been mentioned, and the location of this mountain need not be sought; it lies in the same geographical order as the mountain of temptation (4:8), the mountain of the sermon (5:1), and the mountain of the transfiguration (17:1). The mention of doubt on the part of some is candid (see Jn 20:24–29). Through all the resurrection stories there runs the idea that those who saw Jesus did not recognize him. 19. The apostolic commission is couched in the terms of the experience of the early Church. Brief as it is, it is an unusually clear presentation of what the apostolic Church understood itself to be. The Church acts in virtue of the commission that Jesus has received—a commission that is without limit. By his authority they may make disciples of all nations; there is no longer any question of the restriction of the mission to Jews. *baptizing them:* Their work is to baptize and to teach. Baptism is a rite of initiation; to baptize "into the name" is to signify that the person baptized belongs to the Trinity of persons whose names are invoked in baptism. It seems unlikely that the Trinitarian formula was the earliest baptismal formula employed, and Mt here reflects a more mature practice. 20. The object of the teaching is "all that I have commanded you." This phrase echoes Mt's habitual presentation of Jesus as the new Moses of a new Israel. The word "command" does not affirm the establishment of a new Law, but of a new way of life, just as the Law of Moses established a way of life. *I am with you always:* The final word is an assurance of the living presence of Jesus in the Church, a presence that looks to the eschatological fulfillment of the Church. That Jesus lives in the Church is a belief that is elaborated much more in detail in the Pauline epistles, but it is not an exclusively Pauline idea. The resurrection was not a mere restoration of life nor a mere vindication of the Messiah, but the beginning of a new existence in which the life of the Messiah becomes the enduring life of that group which continues his mission. The Church itself is the witness of the resurrection; for its life and activity are a constant testimonial that Jesus lives.

(Bruce, F. F., "The End of the First Gospel," *EvQ* 12 [1940] 203–14. Dodd, C. H., "The Appearances of the Risen Christ," *Studies in the Gospels* [Fest. R. H. Lightfoot; Oxford, 1957] 9–35. Michel, O., "Der Abschluss des Matthäusevangelium," *EvT* 10 [1950] 16–26. Trémel, V., "Remarques sur l'expression de la foi trinitaire dans l'Église primitive," *LumVi* 29 [1956] 41–66.)

Bibliography

Allen, W. C. *The Gospel According to St. Matthew* (ICC; N.Y., 1907).
Bornkamm, G., G. Barth and H. J. Held. *Tradition and Interpretation in Matthew.* Translated by P. Scott; London, 1963).
Butler, B. C., *The Originality of St. Matthew* (Cambridge, 1951).
Davies, W. D., *The Setting of the Sermon on the Mount* (Cambridge, 1964).
Farrer, A. M., *St. Matthew and St. Mark* (London, 1954).
Fenton, J. C., *The Gospel of St. Matthew* (Baltimore, 1963).
Filson, F. V., *A Commentary on the Gospel According to St. Matthew* (London, 1963).
Gaechter, P., *Das Matthäus Evangelium* (Innsbruck, 1963).
Hummel, R., *Die Auseinandersetzung zwischen Kirche und Judentum im Matthäusevangelium* (Munich, 1963).
Klostermann, E., *Das Matthäus-evangelium* (3d ed.; Tübingen, 1938).
Lagrange, M.-J., *Évangile selon Saint Matthieu* (EBib; 8th ed.; Paris, 1947).
Lohmeyer, E., *Das Evangelium nach Matthäus* (Meyer; Göttingen, 1956).
M'Neile, A. H., *The Gospel According to St. Matthew* (London, 1915).
Schmid, J., *Das Evangelium nach Matthäus* (RNT; 3d ed.; Regensburg, 1959).
Schniewind, J., *Das Evangelium nach Matthäus* (NTD; Göttingen, 1954).
Stendahl, K., *The School of St. Matthew* (Uppsala, 1954).
Strecker, G., *Der Weg der Gerechtigkeit* (Göttingen, 1962).
Trilling, W., *Das wahre Israel* (Munich, 1964).
    F-B 72–86.
    Guthrie, *NTI* 3, 19–48.
    R-F, *INT* 159–90.
Wik, *NTI* 173–99; *IPLCG*, 208–67.

www.ingramcontent.com/pod-product-compliance
Lightning Source LLC
Chambersburg PA
CBHW051101160426
43193CB00010B/1274